COMING TOGETHER:

The Ins and Outs of Liberia's Ups and Downs

COMING TOGETHER:

The Ins and Outs of Liberia's Ups and Downs

ANTHONY BARCLAY

Library of Congress Control Number: 2020902706
ISBN: Hardcover   978-1-7960-8705-5
               Softcover   978-1-7960-8706-2
               eBook   978-1-7960-8715-4

Print information available on the last page.

Rev. date: 02/10/2020

This book is available for sale at Xlibris.com, amazon.com, Ingram Book Distributors, Barnes and Nobel and other distributors available on the internet. It is also available at local book selling places in Liberia. Further, you may contact the author directly at yalcrab77@yahoo.com

To order additional copies of this book, contact:
Xlibris
1-888-795-4274
www.Xlibris.com
Orders@Xlibris.com
776395

Dedicated to

The Liberian People

With a special tribute

to

Mr. Edwin Morgan

**For his confidence in me and mutual
concern for our country, Liberia**

Table of Contents

SECTION ONE: SENTIMENTS OF THE VICISSITUDES OF LIBERIA'S DEVELOPMENT

SECTION TWO: INSIGHTS ON LIFE, RELATIONSHIPS AND RELATED ISSUES WITH SOCIAL AND PHILOSOPHICAL OVERTONES

FOREWORD

Many people are interested in development - what causes the lack of it, the opportunities and challenges, and the success and setbacks in the process of working toward it. Anthony Barclay, the author of this book, *Coming Together: The Ins and Outs of Liberia's Ups and Downs*, poetically speaks about many of these issues in the context of Liberia.

I am one of these people interested in development, Liberia is my home, and the author is my father. Together, our family lived in and out of Liberia. We have a first-hand experience of the country's ups and downs, the good times, and the bad times. Even though I was relatively young growing up in Liberia, I knew when times were good and when they were terrible as it was a shared family experience. My father has dedicated his entire professional life working in the area of development nationally and internationally. With this background, I, being much older now, find it stimulating to discuss with him developmental issues intellectually and sometimes emotionally, as they evolved. I also see our discussion revealing socially in the recollection of conditions as they were during my younger days.

Most importantly, regarding this book, *Coming Together: The Ins and Outs of Liberia's Ups and Downs*, I feel privileged and honored to write the foreword. Generally, the words, phrases, and sentences in each poem provide illuminating awareness of the state of development in Liberia and the potential for progressive change. They encourage Liberians to faithfully and conscientiously participate in the development process positively and to learn from the mistakes of the past.

The poems also include matters of friends and family affairs. It highlights the ups and downs in relationships, primarily love, the birth of children, grief, parental advice, criticism, support, praise, and encouragement. In my judgment, these poems are written so well that they would undoubtedly evoke emotions from the readers.

The messages conveyed are sometimes clear in some poems. In others, they can only be derived through more profound thoughts of not only an appreciation of the lines, rhythm, and style of the poems but also what is implicit between and among the lines.

As a whole, I feel that the book serves as a means of enticing the readers to appreciate his messages of patriotism, honesty and hard work in pursuit of development, personal integrity, commitment, love, and concern for one another. I believe that the poems in this book, like his other poetry books, were written from his heart, mind, and voice. From his heart, a heart that feels the joy and sorrow of Liberia's ups and downs. From his mind, a mind that seeks understanding, empathy, and envisions a better tomorrow. As a voice, the voice of a person providing perspectives of Liberia's development issues and speaking to one another about his understanding and appreciation of family and friendly ties.

I believe reading this book would be a pleasant experience. It could also be a valuable asset of any library, and a useful learning material in the classroom.

Gloria Barclay-Morris
Laurel, Maryland, USA

ABOUT THE AUTHOR

Anthony Barclay is a development specialist and poet. He holds a B. A. in Economics, Cuttington College and Divinity School (currently Cuttington University), Liberia; M. A. in Public Policy and Administration, University of Wisconsin-Madison, USA; and a PhD in Urban and Regional Planning (with a minor in Economics), University of Wisconsin-Madison, USA.

Among other positions he served as Adjunct Lecturer, Cuttington University Graduate School and Professional Studies, Liberia; Senior Advisor to the Executive Director for Africa (Group 1); World Bank, Washington DC, USA; Human Development and Poverty Alleviation Advisor, Economic Community of West African States (ECOWAS), Abuja, Nigeria; Program Officer, African Capacity Building Foundation (ACBF); Harare, Zimbabwe; Executive Director for Research, Policy and Planning, Central Bank of Liberia; Economic Specialist, UNDP, Liberia; Director, of the Office of Planning and Institutional Development and Assistant Professor, University of Liberia; Development Specialist, Liberia Institute of Public Administration.

His publications include:

- Consolidating Peace through Governance and Regional Cooperation: The Liberian Experience. [in Adebayo Adedeji (ed.), Comprehending and Mastering African Conflicts: The Search for Sustainable Peace and Good Governance. London and New York: ZED Books, 1999].

The Political Economy of Brain Drain at Institutions of Higher Learning in Conflict Countries: Case of the University of Liberia. [African Issues, New Jersey, USA: African Studies Association Press, Rutgers, The State University of New Jersey. Vol. XXX/1 2002].

The Political Economy of Sustainable Development: The Governance Perspective. [in Gedeon Mudacumura et al. (Eds.) Sustainable Development Policy and Administration. New York: CRC Press LLC, 2006].

Regional Economic Commissions and Intra-Regional Migration Potential in Africa: Taking Stock. [In Aderanti Adepoju (ed) International Migration: Within, to and from a Globalized World. Ghana: Sub-Saharan Publishers, 2010].

Liberia: Historical Reflections Through Selected Independence Day Orations, 1855 – 2000. [Ed] ; (2017).

Liberia in Thoughts and Plans and other Poems; (2003).

Personal Human Decency: the PHD from the University of Life; (2011).

The Evolution of Central Banking in Liberia (forthcoming).

ACKNOWLEDGMENTS

Several persons, in and out of Liberia, rendered assistance and influenced me in the writing and production of this book. It is practically impossible to name everyone. I am grateful to all. That, notwithstanding, I am obliged to mention a few.

I am particularly thankful to Dr. Emanuel and Mrs. Bella Wariebi-Barclay, Mr. Kenneth and Mrs. Wiatta Princess Barclay-Wilcox and Mr. Samuel and Mrs. Gloria Wiltoinette Barclay-Morris for their hospitality. These people graciously allowed me to use their homes and facilities in New York, Georgia, and Maryland, respectively in the USA while I was away from home in Liberia. In fact, their homes, over varied durations, became my thinking and writing studios. This book would have been impossible without their generosity at a critical time in the process of writing some of the poems, researching, compiling and finally arranging the materials for this book.

I also thank Mr. Willard Baby Ford, Jr. and Ms.Agnes Mial-Fennie, Ms. Patience Wiltoinette Ford, Mr. Matthew and Mrs. Jartu Elious, Mr. Aaron Raphael and Mrs. Bernice Acolatse-Barclay, Mr. Joe and Mrs. Wokie Mai Weah, Mrs. Darcy Cooper Augustus, Mrs. Marrian Wilson and Mr. Rimisa Williams, his family and friends of his family and mine for the opportunity to spend cherished time to relax and socialize during my break from the "book work". Similarly, I sincerely appreciate and thank my children, and all other family members, friends and professional colleagues in Liberia and the United States, for meeting with me socially. These meetings helped me, not only to further relax, but also to motivate me to complete the work, which had been in process for so long. Further, I thank my copyeditors and publishers for their contributions to the final production of the book.

Lastly, I would be absolutely remiss if I did not mention my wife Joyce. Her unwavering exemplary support and understanding was overwhelming in so many ways. I thank her profusely.

The future is now before us – measurably in our own hands – and its character will depend upon the way we now act. If we act a judicious and patriotic part...Liberia will become a political organization deeper in its foundation, wider in its scope and loftier in its significance than it has ever been. And in our various fields of labor, instead of crippling one another through jealousy, we shall stimulate one another to zeal and activity; and we shall bring about a movement on this part of the world such as it has never witnessed...

Dr. Edward Wilmot Blyden

Former Liberian Ambassador to France and the UK, Former President of Liberia College, (precursor to the University of Liberia) and former Presidential Candidate in 1885.

Source: Liberia Independence Day Oration, July 26, 1867, in Anthony Barclay, (ed) *Liberia: Historical Reflections Through Selected Independence Day Orations 1855 – 2000,* Outskirts Press, 2017.

All I have said is, no nation has ever been able to establish and maintain a strong government with a poor ignorant population. Much of [Liberia's] progress in the future will depend on the rapidity with which we mass educate our people now"

Honorable Didwho Twe

Former Member of the House of Representative (1927-1929) and Liberian Presidential Candidate in 1952

Source: Liberia Independence Day Oration, July 26, 1944, in Anthony Barclay, (ed.), _Liberia: Historical Reflections Through Selected Independence Day Orations 1855 – 2000,_ Outskirts Press, 2017.

> "*Of course, we have lived through our historical myths. But we have also recently experienced the empowering spirit of coming together - of standing together; of being more than just the geography that is a country. We have seen the force of a nation - the collective will of a people to overcome, and to survive. We have seen that each of us owes a duty to the other. We have seen that each of us can play a role wherever we are and whatever our station ... becoming increasingly aware of our differences, but looking beyond, and working through our differences, for the common good of all others. We are more than a country - the geography of land blessed with rivers and lakes and monsoon. We are people. We are Liberians - a special people blessed with the gift of resilience ... So, this, truly, is who we are. This is our DNA, which is laden with a resilient character. We no longer have to accept that we cannot come together ...*"

Ministry of Information, Cultural Affairs and Tourism

Source: "We Are Liberians: A Special Statement from the Ministry of Information, Culture Affairs and Tourism (Liberia) Date:5/6/2015. http://RMLiberia/Apps\ SARMMS.nsf/O/F4A554F7C2936A6500257E3DOO38F94B

"For my part, I am a Liberian first and last and my desire is that Liberia should endure till the heavens fall, that this country be controlled by Liberians for Liberians. But I also desire that Liberians be tolerant; that they be prescient; that they be energetic, industrious and public-spirited; that they be courageous in shouldering their national responsibilities; that they be liberal and that they become a great and glorious people, unanimous in sentiment, united in action, abounding in all the virtues which make a nation powerful, perpetual and enduring."

H. E. Edwin J. Barclay

President of the Republic of Liberia, 1930-1944

Cited in Carl Patrick Burrowes, *Power and Press Freedom in Liberia, 1830-1970: The Impact of Globalization and Civil Society on Media Relations, 2004.* See also, Frederick Starr, *Liberia: Description, History and Problems.* Chicago:1913.

"Let us walk the path of nation-building together, looking beyond our individual needs and differences, and embracing the values of citizenship...In declaring our Decade of Peace, let us proudly proclaim - from the Wologisi Mountains of Lofa, and the bounding heights of Nimba, from the cascading Kpatawee Falls of Bong, from the mighty Cavalla River of Maryland, and from the serenity of Lake Piso of Cape Mount - let us loudly proclaim that we are proud to be Liberians!"

"Ethnicity should enrich us; it should make us a unique people in our diversity and not be used to divide us.

H. E. President Ellen Johnson Sirleaf

President of the Republic of Liberia, 2005 - 2017

Source: Speech at the celebration of the 10th Anniversary of the signing of the Comprehensive Peace Agreement (CPA) on August 19, 2013.(See https://tlcafrica. com/news_10_years_of_peace_celebration_august_2013.htm) For the second quote see https://www.quotetab.com/quotes/by-ellen-johnson-sirleaf.

"I have a vision that soon all Liberians at home and abroad will turn to helping and supporting one another instead of turning on and against each other. I have a vision that we will study war no more but instead engage and absorb ourselves in nation building through production, trade, savings, and investments"

Dr. A. Romeo Horton

**Founder and Presiding Officer of the
Bank of Liberia, Liberia's first indigenous banking institution**

Source: Liberia Independence Day Oration, July 26, 2000, in Anthony Barclay, (ed), *Liberia: Historical Reflections Through Selected Independence Day Orations 1855 – 2000,* Outskirts Press, 2017.

"There is no better time to hold together than now. Let our actions speak to the soul of the nation's survival. Let us put aside envy. Let's us together build the Liberia we desire to see... A Liberia that gives our children hope. A Liberia that brightens the smile of a woman in labor and a father on the plantation. A Liberia that ensures that our schools are opened; one that allows you to drive to Maryland and back without an ounce of worry about the roads. Our collective approach MUST change. If we hope that Liberia will be transformed into an oasis of love in the desert of hate."

Hon. David Kolleh

Assistant Minister for Technical Services, Ministry of Information, Cultural Affairs and Tourism

Source: Rodney D. Sieh, "The Fahngon Aftermath", *Front Page Africa.* May 8, 2019. (https://frontpageafricaonline.com/news/liberia-fahngons-aftermath-presidents-surrogates-grounded-in-congau-country-row/)

INTRODUCTION

This is a poetry book. Literary professionals consider poetry to be the most intense form of literature, through which the importance of society, nation building, and development are well documented.[1] Poetry allows writers to express their deepest emotions, thoughts, and concerns in a personal manner, relying on both figurative and literal language as well as rhythm and imagery to convey their messages to readers.[2] Besides these views, the author considers poetry as another suitable medium of scholarship for expressing his views on Liberia's development. He believes that studying poetry, evaluating its messages, and embracing them within relevant contexts can help us in several ways. For example, it can offer us a way to empathize with and support one another rather than in indulging in acts of violence and destruction. He also believes that it can help us in realizing the true essence of a line in the lyrics of the Liberia's national anthem, which says, "in union strong success is sure."

Further, paraphrasing Alice Osborn and adding to her statement, poetry, in its immediacy, is a counselor helping us to understand one another. Poetry helps us move from hate to love, from violence to non-violence, and from underdevelopment to sustainable

---

[1] https://www.reference.com/world-view/importance-literature-society-1a66a3cd21a90dd8. Accessed December 2019 and Kristy Littlehale, Poetry Genres. See https://www.storyboardthat.com/articles/e/literary-genres. Accessed December 2019.

[2] Ibid.

development beneficial to all Liberians.[3] Further, as Kennedy observed, "when power leads [people] toward arrogance, poetry reminds [them] of [their] limitations. When power narrows the areas of [people's] concern, poetry reminds [them] of the richness and diversity of [their] existence. When power corrupts, poetry cleanses for art establishes the basic human truths, which must serve as the touchstones of our judgment … If sometimes our great artists have been the most critical of our society, it is because their sensitivity and their concern for justice, which must motivate any true artist, make them aware that our nation falls short of its highest potential."[4]

This book presents poems that cover some of the salient issues of the Liberian developmental process, highlighting the conditions of progress, stagnation, and retrogression. It is noteworthy that among the many reasons that define each context, human resources are usually paramount. Liberia is constrained by inadequate human resources required for the developmental process. The human resource inadequacy is not only in terms of capacity but attitude and behavior as well. In the context of this book, capacity connotes the ability, fitness, or competency to perform a specified range of tasks or functions. Attitude refers to mindsets; i.e., how a person thinks or feels about someone, something, and a particular situation. Behavior refers to the manifestation of these mindsets through actions.[5]

The author believes that Liberia requires development that is dynamic and sustainable. The manifestation of this development should reflect enhanced national unity, social cohesion, social and economic justice, and political stability. He believes that the people should be more patriotic and self-confident as well as "united in

---

[3]   Alice Osborn, Why is Poetry Important to Our World Today. https://aliceosborn. com/why-is-poetry-important-to-our-world-today/ Accessed December 2019.

[4]   John F. Kennedy, culled from a Speech at Amherst College, USA in honor of the late poet, Robert Frost, The Atlantic, February 1964.

[5]   www.differencebetween.net/language/difference. Accessed December 2019

actions, abounding in all the virtues that make a nation powerful, perpetual and enduring."[6]

The envisioned state of Liberia can be realized when there is an enabling environment for nurturing self-reliance and Personal Human Decency (PHD). This PHD is not necessarily achieved through academic institutions. It is rather achievable through the University of Life, which is naturally and freely accessible to everyone. As stated in another publication, human decency mainly reflects the symbiotic concepts of human dignity and integrity. It postulates that there are influencing linkages between one's human decency and a country's socioeconomic and political challenges and opportunities. In essence, it contends that development is as much a matter of societal attitude and behavior as it is of other relevant factors. These factors include political will, economic systems, institutions, natural endowment, and capacity, among others.[7] Such PHD, infused with exemplary dedication, honesty, and hard-working disposition, is essential to the process of realizing the envisioned Liberia.

Further, the envisioned Liberia, in concert with the PHD, can be achieved through action-oriented policies that support a politically democratic society with the proclivities to be tolerant and caring. Moreover, the requirement for the envisioned Liberia necessitates an equitably progressive economy. While welcoming foreign investors, the Liberian people should be in full and productive possession of the economy that is competitively dynamic and bolstered by resilience and perseverance.

---

[6]   Edwin J Barclay, cited in Carl Patrick Burrowes, *Power and Press Freedom in Liberia, 1830-1970: The Impact of Globalization and Civil Society on Media Relations,2004.* See also, Frederick Starr, *Liberia: Description, History and Problems.* Chicago: Starr 1913.

[7]   Anthony Barclay, *Personal Human Decency: The PhD from the University of Life.* USA: Xlibris, 2011.

There is a saying that there are three (3) ways to do things in Liberia: the right way, the wrong way, and the "Liberian way." Seemingly, the Liberian way is being repeatedly recycled without the desired results. The author supports King-Akerele's view that it is time to break the cycle of the Liberian way.[8] This view is poignantly relevant if the Liberian way is not producing development that is dynamic and sustainable for Liberia. In general, most of the poems in this book advocate for and support all legitimate, innovative, and pragmatic methods and means of achieving the envisioned dynamic and sustainable development discussed above.

The book comprises two sections. In the first section, most of the poetry deals with the author's view of Liberia and expresses, figuratively, in some poems and literally in others, his sentiments and hopes for positive change now and in the future. It also includes his opinions of the human resource factor with a focus on people's attitudes, behaviors, and capacities. It further covers brief historical accounts of the amalgamation of people into the geographical area

---

[8]   Olubanke King-Akerele. The Liberian Way: Breaking the Cycle – The "Growing"of Liberia's Emergent Leadership. Charleston, SC: CreateSpace and Monrovia: Liberian Institute for "Growing" Patriotism and the Angie Brooks International Centre (ABIC) for Women's Empowerment, Leadership Development, International Peace and Security, 2016.

now called Liberia. Besides a few, recent research publications,[9] aspects of these accounts are inadequately covered or not covered in most textbooks used in Liberia's schools today. These aspects include the issues of slavery and its inhumanities, and the people's quest for freedom before the US-based repatriates return to the area now called Liberia. The aspects also include the enormous constraints they faced in nation-building and development after their return and their shortcomings. The above situation also apply to those who virtually faced similar constraints from the West Indies, other parts of Africa and the world, invariably referred to as emigrants, settlers and returnees, who later joined the US-based repatriates. The situation further applies to, those local inhabitants, who joined the new Liberian nation. Each of these groups of people in the new nation faced major constraints and had shortcomings in the process of nation-building and development. These issues are also not adequately covered in several other publications that recycle the often-incomplete account of Liberia's history and socio-economic development.

This first section provides a window into the past and present. Among other things, it highlights the judiciousness, perceptiveness, and resourcefulness of Liberians that contributed to the country maintaining its sovereignty, as well as, the national developmental progress and resilience. It also highlights the mistakes, mis-directions

---

[9] The few recent research publications referred to include the following: Clarence E. Zamba Liberty, Growth of the Liberian State: An Analysis of its Historiography. Northridge, California: The New World Press, 2002; Elliot Berg, "Politics, Privilege, and Progress in Liberia." Liberian Studies Journal, 2 (2), pp 173 – 183; C. Patrick Burrowes, The Americo-Liberian and Other Myths. A Critique of Political Science in the Liberian Context, Temple University, Occasional Papers, No. 3, 1989; Teah Wulah, The Forgotten Liberians: History of the Indigenous Tribes. Bloomington, Indiana: Author House, 2005; C. Patrick Burrowes, Between the Kola Forest and the Salty Sea: A History of the Liberian People Before 1800. Bong County, Liberia: Know Yourself Press, 2016; C. Patrick Burrowes, Liberia & the Quest for Freedom: The Half That Has Never Been Told. Bong County, Liberia: Know Yourself Press, 2019.

and other setbacks, caused either by malfeasance, misfeasance, or nonfeasance, that contributed to the country's developmental stagnation and retrogression.[10]

The second section expresses the author's sentiments and views about family, friends, and a family-connected institution. It also includes poems with philosophical and social overtones. The poems in this second section provide advice and touch upon heartfelt concerns, congratulatory remarks, appreciation, love, sympathy, and empathy in specified contexts. These poems also resonate with the topical issues of the book, "coming together" and "the ups and downs" in the process, i.e., births, deaths, and other life's challenges, progress, and pleasantries in nurturing friends and family relationships.

Finally, the author hopes that this book appeals to not only poets, but others interested in Liberia's development as well as students and the general public inclined toward digesting poetic food for thought. Further, the author trusts that the readers will appreciate this book for its sentimental and educational value.

---

[10] Misfeasance: any act that is illegal or wrongful; Malfeasance: any action that is legal but performed in an unlawful or harmful manner; Nonfeasance: a failure to responsibly act that results in harm or injury.

Section One:

Sentiments of the Vicissitudes of Liberia's Development

Coming Together

Coming together during
Liberia's ins and outs and ups and downs
Will make its people stronger,
Make them successfully climb the development ladder,
And there, at the top, they will all gather
To enjoy the fruits of the struggle,
To enjoy everything that development offers
Upon coming together,
And staying that way forever.

I Know Liberia

I know Liberia,
A Liberia once called the sweet land of liberty
But with its share of bitter calamities.

I know Liberia,
A Liberia once called a land of growth without development
But with elements of progress and enlightenment.

I know Liberia,
A Liberia once called a land of civil wars and anarchy
But with resilience, it overcame the painful brutality.

I know Liberia,
A Liberia once called a severely Ebola-infected nation
But with a strong will, it faced the challenges despite the
limitations.

I know Liberia,
A land striving to have a "wholesome functioning society"[11]
Totally involved with dedication to meet challenges in their
entirety.

I know Liberia,
The ins and outs of its ups and downs—
I know Liberia; I know Liberia.

---

[11] Culled from President Tolbert's policies pronouncements geared towards "creating a wholesome functioning society", Executive Mansion, "Presidential Papers – Documents, Diary and Record of Activities of the Chief Executive", First Year of the Administration of President William R. Tolbert, Jr., July 23, 1971 – July 31, 1972 (Monrovia; N.Y.).

We Must Say It Anyway

We must say it anyway—
Development in Liberia
Defined by criteria
Is a goal worth attaining;
This goes without saying.
But we must say it anyway,
We must say it anyway.

We must say it anyway—
That development in Liberia
Has caused some hysteria
Due to grave misperceptions,
Greed and gross mis-directions.
This truth is often hard to say
But we must say it anyway.

We must say it anyway—
Development in Liberia
In each and every area
Is not easy, is not free;
The fact is there for all to see
But we must say it anyway,
We must say it anyway.

We must say it anyway—
Development in Liberia
Should always be fair
To everyone; big and small;
This is clear to one and all
But we must say it anyway,
We must say it anyway.

Oh Liberia

Oh Liberia, Oh Liberia!
Our mother and father's land;
Our riches outnumber the grains of sand
On the vast scenic coastal landscape
But it's so hard from poverty to escape.
Despite all the development reforms,
We are like a boat in a turbulent storm
Oh Liberia, Oh Liberia.

Oh Liberia, Oh Liberia!
There are many people who are good
And always in a developmental mood;
Working so hard, doing their fair share
While some in high places seem not to care.
Despite the hard times and basic things people lack,
Complaints are like water falling on a duck's back.
Oh Liberia, Oh Liberia.

Oh Liberia, Oh Liberia!
There are people who want to make progress
But they don't know how; conditions regress,
Pride and politics obscure the way forward
In the midst of gravy seekers and cowards.
As bad as it seems, everything is not lost,
These are lessons to learn despite the cost.
Oh Liberia, Oh Liberia.

Liberia to Rise to a Higher Stage

In Liberia's developmental pursuit, we have been led and misled
Along rugged and smooth paths upon which we often tread;
That explains why Liberia has experienced ups and downs.
But let not our spirit and hopes be dampened,
In life, such things from time to time do happen;
As the saying goes, sometimes you'll feel high,
So very high that you can even touch the sky
Sometimes, you'll feel low, lower than the ground
So, my fellow Liberians, don't always wear a frown—
Smile often and act like you'll soon be wearing a crown!
Liberia has vast potential despite its age
Use this potential for Liberia to rise to a higher stage.

Liberia will be here Forever

Like a small lighted candle
Placed in something without a handle,
There was this spark
That lit up the dark
In the Independence Movement Park,
Bringing forth a nation—
The Liberian Nation.
Liberia will be here forever;
It will not be forsaken, no, never!

With all its ins and outs
Amidst those filled with doubts,
Bright have its lights been kept aglow,
Stronger and stronger will it grow.
From diversity, there'll be unity, more and more;
And as winds of crisis challenge this unity,
Liberia will prevail with style and dignity.
Liberia will be here forever;
It will not be forsaken, no, never!

Even with its ups and downs,
Down like a king who lost his crown,
Down as when the people suffered and bled,
Down as when its so-called good friends fled,
Liberia finds ways to move ahead
Like a plane through darkened clouds,
Through distracting noise, unyielding and loud,
Liberia will be here forever;
It will not be forsaken, no, never!

Togetherness for Change and Development

Come together to understand
The ins and outs of Liberia's ups and downs
In search of change for development.
Let's come and stay together
To meet our people's legitimate demands
For the ultimate good of the nation.
Let experience influence our imagination,
But let imagination exceed our experience
To surpass our expectations
Of being exceedingly innovative
Without being exploitative.
In visions, plans, and actions
Everything bad should be raised
Everything good should be praised   .
In search of change for development
Be responsible, with accountability and integrity,
Hold onto honor with agility to the best of your ability.
Let's come together to understand
The ins and outs of Liberia's ups and downs
In search of change for Liberia's development.

Survival in Liberia's Political Landscape

Shifting through the shades
Of dark and bright,
Wrong and right
In Liberia's political landscape,
And learning from the ins and outs,
Gaining experience of what life's about
Will help us survive the ups and downs
In Liberia's political landscape.

Liberia is Upward Bound

Liberia is upward bound
Amidst challenges galore,
Like separating grains of rice
And counting them one by one
The upward struggles continue
Never-ending as the waves of the ocean;
Liberia is upward bound.

In One Way or Another

Liberia's ups and downs
Are our successes and failures
Because the successes positively impact us
In one way or another
Because the failures negatively impact us
In one way or another.
> Liberia's ins and outs
> Are what we should travel through
> In one way or another
> Searching for opportunities
> In all the world's communities.
>> In one way or another
>> To help Liberia reach the highest heights,
>> The upper rooms of life all around
>> And avoid going to the lowest depths,
>> The darkest parts of the underground.

Liberia to Higher Heights

In the struggles of long ago and in the struggles, we face right now
Liberia is for all of us, no matter which
path we, in yesteryears, trod;
We have overcome many tremendous odds.
Liberia is for all of us, no matter which path today we tread
In all that we have been told and all that we have read,
We must find out what's true and what's half true
and explore them further to uncover the pure lies—
Lies spread around like infected flies.
Since the dawn of our history, guided away from the prophetic plan
To build a nation with liberty, justice, and
progress flowing throughout the land.
We have all made mistakes, we have all at times been wrong—
Every social group, every community, every tribe and every clan.
Some people stumbled and fell; some
with painful cries moved along
To carry Liberia to higher heights—every child, woman and man.
We must learn lessons from those who
fell and those who moved on;
Together we must continue the struggle
and believe our national song—
"In union, strong success is sure"; we will prevail.
With a focus on the present and future, let us do whatever it entails
To carry our Liberia to higher heights
Liberia is for all of us; that's a self-evident truth, despite our fights,
And as we celebrate our transition from brutal war to blessed peace
Much more needs to be done to the progress we've achieved.
Let's build on this together with all our might
To carry our Liberia to higher heights.

We Walk Together Side by Side

We walk together side by side
And sing, "All hail Liberia hail,"
Declaring our resolve to never fail,
To work for Liberia's development
Our dear country, our love, our pride.

We walk together side by side
After overcoming our war years,
The sorrow, the pain, and tears.
In union strong, for development;
The pursuit of this goal, we must abide.

Appealing Sentiments

I feel the winds of change all around
With potential wealth for all abound
But I'm sorry to say that there is no change
Except the wind moving to and fro
Tearing down leaves, trees, and more.

        Everything seems to need rearranging
        To ensure that things, for good, are changing,
        To make Liberia move fast, upward bound.
        People are crying; hear their wailing sounds—
        What must be done to turn Liberia around?

What are the reasons for people wailing?
Why is the political economy so badly failing?
Why is this so in a land with vast potential?
Below are some answers my friend has found
In a research he considers empirically sound.

        The reasons were many and by no means hidden,
        As noted below, they were clear but morally
        forbidden:
        "Egotistically driven political power disposition"
        "Greed-dominated vision with violence-prone
        determination"
        "Inexperience and incompetence in heated
        competition"

In simple terms, it means that most people in power
Work every week, every day, hour by hour
To become more powerful and wealthy, first and foremost
By hook or crook, under the table, behind pillars or posts;

Many of these people don't know and pretend that they know
And many don't know and don't know that they don't
How to make this land a better place for all

        Some people have good intentions but don't realize
        the stakes,
        Actions done in good faith may lead to socio-
        economic mistakes.
        From the outside looking in, they make promises to
        do so much,
        But the challenges are not easy and should never be
        considered as such.
        With lofty promises they know not how to deliver
        or manage;
        Their ignorance and greed could result to increasing
        economic damage,
        And the use of needless violence lead to socio-
        political carnage.

Not heeding this caution would place Liberia on its own
To pick up what's lacking, piece by piece
With no concern that Liberia may lose its hard-won peace.
Does this mean these Liberians are failing to learn
From the same things that caused the nation to take a downturn
And lose the peace; that should be our main concern
Let's work together so that the crisis we saw never returns.

        Thanks to those who are not in this narrow-minded
        greedy category
        And those who are, despite the odds, trying to
        safeguard Liberia's glory
        While not perfect, they are trying to reduce the
        country's worries
        By doing the right things, going the right way—yes,
        taking the right stand

To maintain the peace for Liberia, our country, our home, our cherished land.
Together let's say no to losing our hard-earned peace,
In any way, shape, or form for all Liberians to be pleased.
The "union strong" goal should be of the utmost demand
Let us all, from everywhere, join the Development Band.

No Place Else Can We Call Our Own

Liberia, Liberia our beloved home,
No place else can we call our own.
What guides us through the ins and outs
Of Liberia's ups and downs
In every city, village, and town?
Is it the darkness like the forest at night
Where people do things out of sight?
Is it the full moon seen as our village light
When the children play hide and seek
And the adults disappear to do something else?
With all the things that cause our ups and downs,
Sometimes so far down that it causes us to frown,
Let's not despair; we must address all causes of alarm.
So, as we said in our early school days, the "es so so"
"Is he (she) to go in … no, no, he (she) is to go on ... on, on we go." [12]
But I say, let us go on in the right direction without mistakes,
Let's do this for our land, for our beloved Liberia's sake.
Liberia has been and will always be our natural home
There is no place else we can really call our own

---

[12]   Reference to the "es so so" in a similar development context used here was initially used by Dr. Toga Gayewea McIntosh.

Keeping Peace, Development, and Patriotism Alive

We find it difficult to forget the war—
Our civil war of several years ago.
We find it difficult to forget the perpetrators
Who caused the suffering and death we saw.
We must thank God for all the peacemakers,
And now with peace, sweet peace, in place,
Even if the war memories we can't erase,
Including thoughts of those who were killed
Or inhumanely displaced,
The erosion of capacity and skills,
Even if we can't sometimes understand why
We often seem careless and not conscious,
Why we engage in acts that are, to Liberia, so grievous
Why we do what we do to each other, including killing,
Why many joined war gangs—though some were not so willing.
In any case, we must openly admit we went astray
And the path we took carried us far away
From the solutions to our problems still at bay,
Away from our dreams for decency in work and play.
But we are strong and resilient; we must change our ways—
We must now do what we can and even more,
We must reconcile with those full of guilt,
Who destroyed most of what we, together, had built.
We must now stop accusing and casting blame
Without being constructive for the forward way,
With a commitment to never go back again.
We must now stop spoiling good people's names
And stop being jealous of what they have gained
Through hard work, integrity, and other virtues.
Such attributes should be a part of our own menu
And much more to get our desired fame.

Empty criticisms should not be the name of our game—
The past is gone; even though, for some parts, we are ashamed.
Right now, we must help build upon whatever remains;
The future is ours, and toward our desires we can change.
Our past injustice we should rearrange
For good, better, best and thereby never be shortchanged.
After all, when everything is said and done,
We are all Liberians, and we are one!
Even though some have tried to divide the rest of us,
Creating more problems and resolving none,
Leaving us with nothing but fuss and more fuss,
We are one people, one nation; we have a common destiny,
And as such we will remain for eternity,
Building a new and stronger stage
Devoid of injustice, hate, greed, and rage
To keep peace, development, and patriotism alive
And pave the way for all good things to arrive.
For God's sake let this be our aim
So that Liberia's Lone Star will never go dim—
Let's keep peace, development, and patriotism alive.

The Party for Poverty Demise

As they say, "good food should never go to waste,"
Like the Liberian food cooked to our taste,
satisfying the Liberian appetite.
It requires certain ingredients
To make it taste just right,
Giving our bodies good nutrients
At the party for poverty demise.

Economic growth and shared prosperity
As national goals sought in unity,
Long have they wet the Liberian appetite;
They too require the right ingredients,
Like good work and being morally upright,
Like effective leadership and good governance,
Socio-cultural and religious tolerance,
Opportunities and shared responsibility,
At the party for poverty demise.

Education, health, and related services with easy accessibility,
Energy, communication, and transportation infrastructure,
Productivity in mining, manufacturing, and agriculture,
Benefits to be realized therefrom with broad-based equity
Within the realms of realistic possibilities—
Where all contribute to and eventually enjoy
At the party for poverty demise.

I Know A Country

I know a country; I know a country.
It has been to hell and back.
Now, its people stand united,
A torch of glory ignited,
Displaying a flame of determination
In the cause of the Liberian nation,
With a development focus intact
To always work for what it lacks.
It is a challenge, and that's a fact
As the world is not just white or black.
This country I know, I know for sure,
That its people will now ensure
They never, ever, return to war
As they for over fourteen years saw
The futility of it all.

The Elections Visit

With high hopes, we went together to visit
Liberia, our nation, our home
During election time.
O what a feeling; we felt so fine!
But it turned acrimonious and violent
O what a disappointment
Elections without civility!
Elections without sanity!
Mr. Integrity, where were you and Miss Dignity?
Lost in the valley of innate dishonesty
Or in an asylum of temporary insanity?
Was it so disguised that the fraud we could not find?
Or was it a case of suspicious, selfish, destructive minds?
Will we ever know; will we ever know for sure?
In clear daylight, everywhere, what will the truth show?
While we wait for answers, we return from our visit.
We must do our utmost best, with God's help, to deposit
Virtues of magnanimity and decency in our characters
It will make a difference; it will truly matter—
For the good of everyone, the good of our nation,
During elections and always, for the good of our nation.

The Imperative for Peace

The imperative for peace
In Liberia, our Liberia
Is what we've always preached.
May the process not be breached
Even with the usual noise.
We must in peace vote our choice,
And then the people would have spoken,
Not as a mere token
Or something good for nothing
But as a binding stance
In all and every circumstance
Not ever to be broken
To help us in remaking
One people, one nation
Of God's own creation.
Heed, my people, one and all—
The imperative for peace
Should always be our curtain call
In Liberia, Our Liberia

"In union, strong success is sure"
In Liberia. Our Liberia,
We'll reach our goals; that's ensured.
The real development goals
With relative calm and ease—
The goals that go beyond the polls.
The process may be slow
With challenges galore,
But the imperative for peace
Should never ever be ignored.
For all Liberians to be pleased

Let the elections be fair, I plead
Devoid of power-seeking greed.
Let's put our Liberia first,
And please, let this be our creed.
Heed, my people, one and all,
The imperative for peace
Should always be our curtain call
In Liberia. Our Liberia.

Liberia's Problems and Opportunities

At the beginning of my life,
Trying to know the "why" before the "what" and "how"
Of Liberia's problems and opportunities,
I never understood them, but I thought I did

Now, at the end of my life,
Having been in the hallways and classrooms
of the University of Life
Where I tried to know
And learn what I didn't know
About the "what" and "how" before the "why,"
I understand and know that I do.

And now I wish to seize the opportunities
I wish to address the problems
No one knows everything, but I must act on what I know
About the "what," the "how," and the "why"

Liberia is the way it is, but this way can be changed
If we address what is wrong; if we strive to know how
And if we understand and learn lessons why things went wrong.

Born to be Liberians

We were born to be Liberians.
From wherever we may be returning,
Our hearts must be yearning
For peaceful co-existence
And a livelihood above subsistence.

We were born to be Liberians—
To be outright with each other,
To help one another,
To give our best in serving
Our Liberia that is so deserving.

Introspection

Liberia, beautiful Liberia!
As its people rise and sing
Songs of joy and songs of pain,
Reminiscing historical highlights,
Looking at themselves out and in—
Introspection, that's what it's called,
Clear and plain; clear and plain.

Introspection: What does it say to you and me?
Have we been good or simply mean?
Have we been biased out of ignorance
Or just a show of greedy power play
To win personal and political games
At the end of each and every day?
Introspection, introspection.

We All Cherish the Love of Liberty

We all cherish the love of liberty
In the pursuit of a good life and happiness.
Now, today, at this point in time,
Whether love of liberty brought us here or not
Would coup d'état, civil war, and violent social-ethnic conflict
Bring us relief, resolve problems, meet development challenges
Or are they more prone to divisiveness and self-destruction?

> We know that some of us perpetrated the slave
> trade,
> Selling our people to slavers destined for
> dehumanizing bondage
> Now, today, at this point in time,
> Would coup d'état, civil war and violent social-
> ethnic conflict
> Bring us relief, resolve problems, meet development
> challenges
> Or are they prone to divisiveness and
> self-destruction?

The burning issue today is how to co-exist in peace
For if we are deprived of the love of liberty by fighting among
ourselves,
If we are deprived of our independence by condemning ourselves,
Our freedom to think and take the right actions
With objectivity and emotional intelligence,
Our freedom to evaluate ourselves responsibly
On what we do or don't to best co-exist in peace,
Through the preservation of our liberty and independence.

We'll all become slaves of our own making,
Controlled by perennial ignorance and poverty
And manipulated by greedy power-seeking masters
To the detriment of us all, weakened to our very core
Without our liberty and independence. What a sore; what a sore!

A Tale of a Nation Ruled by Presidents

Once upon a time,
There was a nation ruled by Presidents
Who made promises at every event
To end what's known as corruption.
But they failed in all their actions
So, the people called them "Corrupt-dents"
Rather than the dignified "Presidents"
And the corruption continued at all events,
Badly affecting the nation's development.

The Battle of the Bundles of Confusion

The bundles of confusion
Wrapped in cocoons of seclusion,
Protected by forces of exclusion,
In a battle with forces of inclusion
Within their own bundle of confusion.
With selfish inclinations
To build their own cocoons of seclusion,
All the bundles of confusion
Lead only to the detriment of the nation.

The True Story: The Love of Liberty and the Liberian People[13]

You may not be aware of the whole story
What brought our people together long time ago
Since the story has generally not been factually told
The Mediterranean and the trans-Atlantic Slave trade
Promoted the capture and selling of our people by our people
Those captured were carried far across the ocean and sea to strange
lands
To Europe, the Americas and other areas they had never known
They were enslaved; this fact Liberia's history has not clearly shown

Those captured were treated as animals beneath the human race
What a despicable, devastating and inhumane treatment
Caused by the participation of our own people for their selfish
enrichment
Slavery, such degradation, including sexual assault and grievous
overwork
Led directly to many of the captives' death; others died fighting
Fighting to be free or trying to flee from the yolk of slavery
While many survived, slavery left a devastating toll on their lives
This truth is absent from our history, or distorted as half-hearted
lies

Again, I must stress, the slavery situation was caused by our own
people
Who captured their own kind by kidnapping, unprovoked raids and
other means
And sold their own people into slavery; what a shame; what a
shame

---

[13]   The writing of this poem benefited from C. Patrick Burrowes book entitled:
       Liberia & the Quest for Freedom – The Half That Has Never Been Told,
       already cited in the footnote of the Introduction of this book.

The captors and sellers became empowered from the income
received from the slave trade
From which they derived prestige and more power in their towns
and villages
Causing the capturing and selling to last for many years
Causing distrust and fear to become common among communities
Which has, among other things, contributed to our present-day
disunity

To avert captivity some of our people were forced to migrate
From their Sahelian homes to the vast forest regions
In the area some of which later became known as Liberia
I know today due to several factors most people are not familiar
With the facts of this story, but also know, that after many years
Some of our people's ancestors were set free and repatriated
To the place where Liberia eventually became an independent
nation
Due to many factors, including the migrants and non-migrants'
determination

Later, following the abolition of slavery, people were liberated
Yes, liberated from slave ships by the US and UK anti-slavery
vessels
Dispatched in the area now called Liberia; they became the new
arrivals
Later, other people from the Caribbean, and nearby UK colonies
As well as other parts of this our world, north, south, east and west
Note also that all migrants met others to this place now called
Liberia
This is the story of the amalgamation of people's settlement in this
area.

Thus, in one way or another, whatever you think, say or do
The love of liberty is a main reason we are all here;
The love of liberty brought some here

To escape from the Mediterranean slave trade
To escape from the Transatlantic slave trade;
Love of liberty made some return here
After their ancestors were sold by their own people
The love of liberty made others to come here
In support of the first modern day independent African nation
The love of liberty motivated some not to leave here
Because of the stability and liberty that they enjoyed here
I hope the love of liberty increasingly unites us here
As one people; one nation; one destiny

The love of liberty is important to everyone here,
Whether it brought you here or kept you here;
The love of liberty is a single universal oneness,
It combines us here - one nation, one people
While we may have been divisive at times, to our detriment,
While some who returned treated others grossly unfairly
Today is a new day, a new era and a time for positive change
Let's live the true meaning of humanity; it's long overdue
The true meaning of our national anthem, which says,
"In union, strong success is sure; we will all prevail."

A Nightmare and a Dream

As I traveled to the place called Development
I became weary, so I stopped to rest awhile.
In disbelief, I saw the brain sending
Misleading messages to other parts of the body,
And I saw other parts of the body malnourishing the brain.
I saw these actions, mischievously flawed actions;
I saw these actions, deviously sinister reprisals,
Then, I heard sounds of violence, pain, and suffering.
Later I realized that in my weary state
   I had fallen asleep; what I'd seen and heard were in a
   nightmare.

I continued my travel to the place called Development,
And there I saw the brain and other parts of the body
Struggling with a common vision, a common cause
All with lofty ambitions and sense of direction,
With a development-results orientation
For achieving socioeconomic transformation—
Justice, opportunities for participatory wealth creation,
Shared prosperity, and sustained progression
On a path toward elevating the entire body.
Again, I must have fallen asleep
Because what I saw did not reflect reality
It was only a dream, my dream, my dream.

I then thought, What a difference
Between my nightmare and dream,
if I had to make a choice,
What I'd choose is crystal clear.

Before the New Day Ends

Liberia, Liberia, Liberia,
A land that's filled with diamonds and ore,
Gold and so much more—yes, so much more,
Yet, tell me why most of our people are poor.
The answer can be found in the past
It shows on the faces, sad and cold
It's the wrong we once did that now unfolds.

But today is a new day as the sun rises!
Before this new day ends, before it ends,
There will be pleasant surprises
Through a leadership that cares
And with the people doing their fair share
So do not despair; do not shed tears,

Change is just around the bend.
Good governance and capacity it will bring,
The fruits of our labor will henceforth spring,
And progress will come before the new day ends.
Before the new day ends—yes, before it ends,
Change is just around the bend.

Toward Enjoyment

"In joy and gladness with our hearts united"[14]
Liberians enjoy, enjoy, enjoy and enjoy!
Stop complaining and doing nothing; seek happiness.
I know it is not always easy; life itself is never easy.
Living is tough for so many, like a bottle filled with emptiness;
Sometimes we feel bad, disappointed, and even queasy
As the grass often seems greener on the other side
Amidst frustration to get there, to relax, and to reside.
Sometimes it seems no matter how hard we try,
At the end of the day there are more reasons to cry,
But we must always be grateful for what we have—
Peace, independence, and our freedom as a sovereign nation,
Our spirit to never give up; long live that determination!

I know we need much more to improve our living condition;
Peace, independence, freedom, and determination are not enough.
But they make a strong foundation for our developmental case,
And with this foundation, we can strengthen and widen our base
To reach all sectors of our economy and segments of our population,
Our base on which to work for our present and future generations.
That is called life's enrichment and sustainable development
To strengthen, enhance, and protect independence and freedom.
Just that thought alone is cause for hope and enjoyment—
Enjoyment by working hard; enjoyment by playing for a while.
So, Liberians, "In joy and gladness with our hearts united"
Toward progress, let's dedicate ourselves in every rank and file,
And in the process, enjoy and enjoy in our own Liberian style!

---

[14]   From Liberian National Anthem, "All Hail Liberia Hail"

I Hear Liberia Singing

I hear Liberia singing,
"All Hail Liberia Hail."
I hear Liberia singing,
"The Lone Star Forever."
The melodies, the rhythm, the lyrics
Keep me higher than high,
Not like birds flying in the sky
But high in thoughts on how to take concerted actions;
High in how we, with everyone, can strategically consult
Committed to ensuring we get the right results;
High in words and deeds to gain and maintain the right traction,
Through union strong to uphold Liberia forever,
To never forsake Liberia, no never, no never.

Nightmare in the Middle of that Stormy Night

Somehow, I slept in the middle of that stormy night
You appeared and fought me with all your might,
Destroying yourself and the little I had;
I despised you for what you did was bad,
And I did not know you or from where you came.

Somehow, I awoke and heard you singing my favorite song,
I saw you smile, and that made me sing along,
Happy to know that what happened was not a real fight
The fight I thought we had in the middle of that stormy night—
It was my mind recalling our brutal civil war.

I knew that I had just had a nightmare
That gave me such a terrible scare
In the middle of that stormy night.
Now, I feel like a bird in flight,
Enjoying the free natural air.
Working hard with a development flair

More Than Just Dreams

Liberian dreams, Liberian dreams.
Dreams of progress; such dreams
Will forever and ever remain
Dreams; just dreams
If we sit and refrain,
Refrain from acting to attain
Developmental progress with a passionate flame,
A commitment to always sustain
Through firm words and deeds,
With the valor to proceed
With a progressive transition
From just dreams to purposeful action
For the Liberian nation.

Toward Liberia's Healthy Longevity

You can have zeal and versatility
If you take advantage of opportunities,
If you have an open mind for universality,
If you do the good you do with quality,
If you have a pleasant personality,
If you interact with others with integrity,
If you resolve problems without animosity,
If you help others do their best with alacrity,
If you exercise your rights with responsibility,
If you contribute to improve Liberia's capability.
That way, my fellow Liberians,
You'll be good for eternity,
Leaving Liberia with healthy longevity.

Liberia's Journey to the Place to be

On turbulent seas, rugged roads, high hills, and deep valleys,
From poverty Liberia must escape and find the place to be,
Sometimes in vessels ill-equipped to withstand the waves,
Yet, Liberia is moving toward the place to be; the place to be.
Over hills and valleys, across challenging landscapes,
Sometimes in vehicles ill-equipped to withstand the rugged roads
And exacerbated by other constraints that increase the load,
Yet, Liberia is moving toward the place to be; the place to be.
Tattered and weakened on the outside
But strong and determined on the inside,
In search for peace, justice, and progress for all
Together let's shout out and make the call,
"Keep going, keep going Liberia; keep going!
Onward march, Liberia, onward march,
With the unity and strength of your people,
Every man, woman, and child,
You will over all the obstacles prevail
And reach your noble destiny"
At the place to be; the place to be.
Let's shout out and make the call,
"All hail Liberia, All hail, All hail!"
Together we'll reach the place to be;
The place to be, your noble destiny.
Together, let's shout out and make the call
For peace, justice, and progress for all.

Keeping Liberia From Falling

Let's cast our eyes toward the skies,
Let's walk together, side by side,
Not forgetting that we may be strong,
But that our strength won't last for long
If we forget that we are on the ground,
Living with those who wish we listen to their cries
As they too cast their eyes toward the skies,
To empathize with those whom problems always surround,
To never neglect those who are sick and unable to look around,
To seek help in finding solutions to their plight,
To understand those whose motives are hidden in disguise
But whose intents are somehow seen clearly in their eyes.
Let's help them come out of the dark and face the light
To keep Liberia from falling.

When we cast our eyes
Up toward the skies,
We seek Heavenly guidance
From the Almighty high above
Or wherever else that guidance is with love
To help us help others with style and elegance.

When we walk together side by side,
We put all our differences aside
To work together in unity,
To solve the problems for one and all
So, Liberia will never fall.

A Call to Liberian Patriots

Liberians patriots arise, arise!
Find ways and means to help Liberia;
Be prepared to pay the price,
And make the required sacrifice,
Not necessarily with blood
But with courage and sweat
As one swims against the tidal flood,
Being unafraid in the process to get wet.
That sometimes happens to cause an effect,
Not by merely criticizing and empty talking
But through non-violence and firm posture taking.

Offer solutions to the problems,
Say not only "what" should be done
But how and why the "what" should be done.
Take a stand to promote the opportunity
Do so as best as you can in unity
For "in union strong success is sure";
I am sure you heard that before.
To change the landscape of poverty
In your land, your Liberian land,
Take a stand to reduce inequality.
In your land, your Liberian land,

Avoid revolutions that promise everything;
Many have proven to deliver nothing,
We saw them before; they were destructive
Change your stance; be committed and constructive.
Study and work hard with dignity,
Be honest and manifest integrity,
The struggle for progress has begun.

It's the noblest cause under the sun,
Be steadfast until this noble cause is won.
Liberians patriots arise, arise!
Together we will surely win the prize.

Painting a New Picture of Liberia

If I were an artist ... if I were an artist,
I'd paint a new Liberia, a new Liberia—
A country with a difference,
A beautiful paradise.
Not one that angels inhabit,
Flying around with outstretched wings
Without problems and conflicting issues
But a beautiful land-based paradise
That human beings inhabit,
Walking on solid, soft, and sandy grounds,
Amidst problems and conflicting issues
But where they manifest good habits;
Not to imbibe drinks of greed
But work to meet the country's needs,
Not to languish in prisons of perpetual hate
But shower love and respect, and do all it takes
To resolve problems and conflicting issues

To sustain the new Liberia, the new Liberia.
Along the path to higher heights, higher heights
Nurturing a wholesome functioning society,
A vision that became cloudy in its entirety
On a historical journey many years ago
And even in recent past.

If I were an artist ... if I were an artist,
A picture I'd paint; I'd paint it to last.
The vision would be rekindled,
Everyone would intermingle
With the clarity of the sky on a sunny day.
All will see a country with a difference,

Where there's liberty and justice for all;
Where there's progressive development,
For everyone big and small
Without problem-causing social distinctions—
A paradise inhabited by hard- honest working people;
The Liberian people all around the world
And on the grounds in a new progressive Liberia.

The Fake Story of Liberia's Death

That morning,
Liberia did not get out of bed.
Indigestion perhaps; she may have been overfed
By those who wanted her dead.

The day before,
We heard that she was old, very, very old
And she had no one to care; all her things were stolen or sold
Except the clothes she had on and those were soiled with mold.

That afternoon,
She was an awful sight to behold.
I felt her hands; they were cold, very, very cold.
I asked why, and this is what I was told.

"This evening,
Liberia died.
She is dead; very dead.
We are all afraid."
"Afraid of Liberia's death?" I asked.
They answered, "Yes, afraid!"
I kept these words for long within my aching head.

That night,
I, too, became afraid and was afraid to be afraid
After deep reflection, this is what I said.
"Liberia cannot be dead;
Her hands may be cold, very, very cold,
But she may just be old, very, very old.
She cannot be dead."

The next day,
I said to myself, in my head,
Perhaps Liberia is at rest; let's hope she rests in peace
Away from the noise of this world
The coup d'états and civil wars
That breaks us all up piece by piece
Until we are dead but never *really* dead
Because each one of us is a part of Liberia
In different forms, roaming the country and region,
Trying to go to a place called Development
In Development, Sustainable Development.
Liberia cannot and will not die—
That is what we must work toward,
Making Liberia to move forward
To the place call Development.
The story of Liberia's death was faked
Liberia can never die; this we all must ensure

Put Liberia on the Right Side

We all have different sides.
You are walking alone on the dark side;
You seem so very dissatisfied.
But you can see the bright light outside;
That's where the truth, like sunshine, abides.
And there, absolutely nothing can hide;
Join us on the bright side.

Liberia belongs to the right side.
Leave the dark side, and find the bright side
Where you'll know the inside from the outside.
Come inside, my friend, come inside,
There we may look for the good outside.
But let's bring that good inside
With truth not circumscribed
To strengthen Liberia's bright side;
Come and let us together reside.

To everyone, I say, let's walk side by side
To put Liberia on the right side
Where the truth like sunshine abides—
That's where Liberia belongs; the right side.
Put Liberia there; on the right and bright side.

Liberia: Muddling Through the Logic

You dare say that Liberia is nothing,
And nothing means nothing.
Then, nothing can come out of nothing.
So, something from nothing is nothing.
But something is only something
When considered relative to nothing.
Thus, nothing gives meaning to something
And something is real; it exists.
Liberia exists; Liberia is something.

So how dare you say Liberia is nothing?
Is it because you consider yourself as nothing?
But if you are, it follows from the logic above
That nothing can give meaning to something;
Let's hope that something is you.
Let's hope that you can become a good thing
That can yield many more good things too
To make Liberia everything; everything good
To you, to me, and to everyone with love.

To Give Our All in All

To help this land of ours, Liberia,
Things get done through words and deeds,
And not only by praying to God to meet our needs.
We know that we cannot always do it by yourself;
We may put God first, but we need to also work.
Sometimes, in doing so, we need help from others.
But don't be dependent; let's work together to move further.
The way a plant needs water, sunshine, and food from the soil,
Let us give dear Liberia, the land we love, our all in all.

Liberty for Liberia; Liberia for Liberty

For Liberia, a name that originates
From the Latin word *libertatem,* meaning liberty,
Our liberty we must uphold with courage and integrity;
There should be no room for mediocrity
And certainly not for complacency or apathy.
This notion we must illuminate
As it is said "liberty and justice for all"
Living the meaning from which Liberia's name is derived,
That's what we must do; yes, for that we must stand tall.
Liberty for Liberia; Liberia for liberty.

Let's Keep the Unity in Liberian Community

One wholesome functioning community—
That's the Liberian community that I envisioned,
Where everyone works in union strong together.
Be aware; upon taking **unity** out of comm**unity**
All one is left with is "**comm**," not a word in my dictionary,
But it sounds like come; it sounds like come.
Come and take the good people for granted,
Come with discord and avoid being reprimanded,
Come and steal whatever you greedily wanted,
Come and take the fruits you never planted.
When unity is not in the community,
It is like taking fish out of water
Where it will wiggle until it dies;
Let's keep the **unity** in Liberian comm**unity**
So, the people do not just wiggle until they die.

Liberia is Always on My Mind

I've travelled the world, far and near,
Sometimes in groups, sometimes alone,
Sometimes under conditions to fear.
Throughout it all, happy or sad,
I never stop thinking about my home.

Yes! Liberia is always on my mind
In the search for ways for me to find,
In the world of ideas, and on the ground for action
For this Liberia, my beloved nation,
Is like something in my veins,
Running as blood flows to nourish my brain.
Sometimes ideas flow like never-ending rain,
Sometimes they stop flowing; this causes pain.
But I still see the Liberian people in my dreams;
I see some who think without acting,
I see some who act without thinking.
But throughout it, all happy or sad,
I see their needs; I feel their hopes to help in making
A great Liberia where everyone will be glad
To do things in union strong, together as one.

Yes! One nation, one people, one Liberia;
That keeps Liberia always on my mind.
With high hopes that one day we will find
Some ways and means to do what's best
In the world of ideas, and on the ground for action
For this Liberia, my beloved nation.
This calls for in-depth reflection

With no reprisal for past misdirection.
This calls for a new vision for transformation;
This calls for closer cooperation and action
To work with a positive-results orientation.

Acrostic for Liberia

Love Liberia always; do it in ways that are not faked
Inquire about what needs to be done for Liberia and do it.
Be not discouraged when sometimes you fail.
Every now and then obstacles will come your way.
Rise above the detractors and meet the challenges, night and day.
Innovate to find and apply good strategies to steer Liberia ahead.
Always remember Liberia is your home; do what's right from "A to Zed."

Liberia's Abcdefgarious Poem

Although Liberia, like all countries, lacks perfection
Because of human and other limitations,
Cease not to do your best to help Liberia move in the ideal direction;
Do not hesitate to rest, but loose not your determination.
Enable others along the way with exemplary dedication;
Fear nothing, but don't be stupid, be careful and pay attention,
God helps those who help themselves; remember that with no contention.

If Development Is Your Goal

If development is your goal,
Reprisal may not be the best way to go
Because reprisal breeds reprisals
The impacts of which last, last, and last,
And your goal of achievement stalls;
Be strong and stand with dignity tall,
Learn lessons from your far and near past,
And pursue your goals faster than fast.
But overcome reprisal with a blast
If development is your goal.

Eleemosynary

I am Eleemosynary;
That is my name.
I know it sounds strange;
Look me up in the dictionary,
And don't always be like what it means.
Don't get me wrong, being charitable is good
But living and depending solely on charity
Is not a lifestyle to sustain

The Challenge

Walking in a straight line,
Like taking a sobriety test
I know such walk can be stressful;
Reaching the end progressively in time—
This I know can be called successful.
Success comes when you give your best,
Helping others; not forgetting the rest.

Better Things Are Still to Come

Liberia!
As beautiful as a tricolor rose,
All over we see red, white, and blue;
In a blue field, a lone white star enclosed.
I wonder if the beauty is a clue
That better things are still to come.

In Search of Liberia's True Story

Let's go on a journey to find out
Who knows the true story,
The facts of Liberia's history.
Not only the bits and pieces
Whose sum do not constitute the whole;
I mean the whole truth
And absolutely nothing else
In search of Liberia's true story.
Yes, let's be very clear;
I don't mean the half truths
And certainly not the whole lies
Told by those with hidden agendas
And those out of simple ignorance,
Blinded by misguided arrogance
Whose actions show they care less
About the challenges and progress
That define Liberia's experience;
Encapsulated in its long history,
They tell Liberia's true story.
Let's go in search of Liberia's true story.

For the Love of Liberty

For the love of liberty
In our dear Liberia,
No matter from where we've come,
From nowhere or anywhere,
Today we are Liberians.
For the love of liberty,
Together we must remain
And cherish Liberia,
Remember all those who worked
To make this land a State
In the comity of nations;
Remember all those who cried,
And those who died,
And those blatantly ignored,
Whom we may never know,
In the fight for equal rights,
Justice and security,
Sustainable prosperity—
To make all Liberians
One people, one nation,
Our fight must continue
Against dishonesty and greed.
Indifference, we can't afford,
As ill-gotten wealth is not our creed,
Power abused will not meet our needs;
This should never be ignored.
It is up to me and you
To keep this Liberia
A land for me and you;
One nation, one people.

Facts Matter

Facts about Liberia matter,
About its "this" and "that."
Unless one knows the facts,
It would be most difficult,
If not impossible,
To intelligently say
This is due to that.
When one knows not the "that,"
The times, the conditions, the constraints,
the experience and complaints,
missed opportunities and restraints
And how things have changed
To "this" and the role of "that"
Transforming "that" to "this."
Get to know the facts; they matter
To Liberia's this and that,
And then find out what you can do
To make today's "this" better
Than yesterday's "that."
Know the history,
The whole story;
Understand constraints,
Meet the challenges,
Seize the opportunities.
Facts about Liberia matter—
Facts about this and that,
To make Liberia prevail
No matter what comes in the way.

We Will Overcome No Matter What

The song "All Hail Liberia Hail"
Still sounds around the globe
Despite selfish, manipulative plans
And other ill-attempts to bring and keep us down.
They could not with success do this for long,
Despite sinister, unwholesome debates;
This was simply not Liberia's fate.
Steadfast, we've survived; one people, one nation,
Working together in union strong
With thoughts embedded in our souls
To seek national progress as our goal.
We will all prevail; we will all prevail
As we sing with all our might,
"All Hail Liberia Hail"
And strive to always fight the good fight,
With malice for absolutely none.
With respect for one and all to meet our needs,
We will prevail over those with malice and greed,
And all other ill-intents that stand in our way;
We will overcome no matter what they do or say.

In Liberia's Developmental Process

In Liberia's developmental process,
Some understand the problems,
The magnitude of the task,
While others just simply don't,
And many questions they ask.
Sometimes, we hear things
We may prefer not to hear,
But they have a right to ask;
This must be loud and clear.
We all must search for answers
On our development quest,
Even though with the best efforts
Some people will always protest.
They have a right to that
But let's do that for a good purpose
To move Liberia forward
And not to protest for protesting sake
The people's rights must be protected
We must all have patience,
This our conscience should attest
In this development process.
There should be no reprisals
But only fair actions to redress
Mis-directions, while being aware
That "progress is the best revenge"
For all that went wrong, simple and clear,
In Liberia's developmental process.

The What, How, and Why in the Liberian World

In the Liberian world, all things are seemingly possible.
In the Liberian world, all things are seemingly impossible.
It all depends on our reflections
of what we thought and did and how and why;
it all depends on our mindsets,
what we are now thinking and doing and how and why;
it all depends on our visions
on what we should be thinking and doing and how and why.
In the Liberian world,
The possibility of seeing the impossibilities,
And the possibility of seeing the possibilities,
Rest with me and you,
With our thoughts and actions.
"Is that true or untrue?"
That is a question for me and you
In the Liberian world.

My Love for Liberia

I've seen Liberia fall,
Being kicked around like football
That's when we fought our civil wars
The death and destruction we saw.

I've seen Liberia grow
With the brightest smiles aglow;
I know there is much more to come
Greater will its people become.

In the ups and downs my love remains—
I love Liberia and I'm not ashamed,
My heart and head tell me it's so,
And they never lie; Liberia knows.

Beyond Just Lingering On

The Africans involved in the slave trade are gone;
Liberia still lingers on.
The Arabs involved in the slave trade are gone;
Liberia still lingers on.
The Europeans involved in the slave trade are gone;
Liberia still lingers on.
The Americans involved in the slave trade are gone;
Liberia still lingers on.
Those tribal chiefs and others that aided the slave trade are gone;
Liberia still lingers on.
Those bigoted so-called immigrants are gone;
Liberia still lingers on.
The founding folks with limited capacity to manage a new nation
are gone;
Liberia still lingers on.
Those "progressives", the revolutionaries, who underestimated the
army's NCOs[15] are gone;
Liberia still lingers on.
Those supporters of the revolution who misjudged the aftermath
are gone;
Liberia still lingers on.
The military rule that promised much but delivered little is gone;
Liberia still lingers on.
The warlords and rebels who called themselves "freedom fighters"
are gone;
Liberia still lingers on.

The time is now for all to help Liberia to move beyond
just lingering, lingering, and lingering on.

---

[15]   Non Commissioned Officers

In fact, moving beyond just lingering on is overdue
To move beyond just lingering on, we Liberians must build upon
what's left from just lingering on; the good and the bad, therefrom.
With "no reprisal for the past" and "malice toward none,"
We must accept the adage, "what's done, is done."
Let's focus on security, justice, and progress for everyone.
Those who want revenge, remember, revenge begets revenge;
that's no fun.

The time is now for us all to help Liberia to move beyond
just lingering, lingering, and lingering on.
We must all help move "from mats to mattresses,"[16]
From lower depths "to higher heights,"[17]
And live the true meaning of the words,
"Above all else, the people."[18]

---

[16] Expression from Former President William R. Tolbert.

[17] Expression from Former President William R. Tolbert.

[18] Expression from former President Charles G. Taylor

Liberian Birds Whistled Peace

It was fourteen years ago
Or just a little more,
When the Liberian birds whistled "ee pe pea pea,"
I guess they were trying to whistle "peace,"
A call for all fighting and looting to cease
And adherence to the Accra Peace Conference decrees,
For socio-ethnic rivalry to significantly decrease,
A chance for the good in us to be released,
An opportunity to rebuild Liberia piece by piece
Since everything cannot be done at once with ease;
An imperative with which everyone agrees—
Today, there's progress, but our efforts must increase
So that with peace, development will be achieved
In ways for all Liberians to feel, see and believe
What peace and development can guarantee.

Toward A Beacon of Progressive Enlightenment

For Liberians to meet the challenges of development,
To me, it would be by far more prudent
To distinguish between our needs and wants
And then change our pursuit of what we want;
Like being a beacon of progressive enlightenment
For the strategic pursuit of what we truly need
And the best ways to get and make use of them—
Peace, good governance, and sustainable livelihood
In every city, town, village, and neighborhood,
And justice for all as a part of our creed.

With peace, good governance, and sustainable livelihoods
In every city, town, village, and neighborhood
And ensuring justice for all as a part of our creed
Along with other critical acquired needs
Strategically we can work in pursuit of what we want
Meeting our needs and the way we make use of them
Will pave our path toward a brighter tomorrow,
Enabling us to share our lessons from sorrow
And help others along roads that are bumpy and narrow,
Toward a beacon of progressive enlightenment
And to have justice for all as a part of development.

Hope of the Liberian People

Liberia, I hail you again and again.
Your people hope, and in their slumber, they dream
Of a great nation one day to be acclaimed,
Where bright lights eliminate the darkness seen,
Where selfishness leads to no useful gain,
Where hypocrisy will end with stinging pain,
Leaving the lack of integrity unhidden and plain,
Replaced with hard work, honesty and a lifestyle clean.
Liberia, I hail you again and again.

Making This Nation Strong

What can be done to make this nation strong,
To thrive along paths that are rugged and long,
Toward goals called sustainable progress for all
So that this nation will not again fall?

Is it not riches like diamond and gold?
Is it not riches like rubber and ore?
Is it not riches like good prospects for oil?
Is it not the good agricultural soil?

These riches are good but not enough,
Making this nation substantively tough
Needs hardworking folks with capacity—
People with honor and integrity.

Strengthening this, our beloved nation,
Needs nothing like the scrooge of corruption;
We need to fight it with good words and deeds
To change the mindsets of those filled with greed.

For Development in Liberia

For development in Liberia,
We all need to contribute.
No longer can we sit and wish;
It is not a free-for-all endeavor.
There is always a price to pay,
And we should pay our fair share
Toward Liberia's development.
No longer can we just brush off
The dishonesty and greed,
Lust for wealth and power,
And put on the bigshot show;
Such acts will not meet Liberia's needs.
This should be made clear for all to see—
We all must contribute, and on this we must agree;
Let this not be simply you, them, or me.

Keep Liberia In Your Mind and Heart

For every good thing you do,
Keep Liberia in your mind and heart;
Remember you were a significant part,
A part of Liberia from the start.
While you may have moved from here to there,
Always show that you truly care,
By giving your share, your fair share,
To Liberia whether you are here or there.
As we celebrate this Holiday season,
There are so many concrete reasons
To keep Liberia in our minds and hearts.

Dreaming of Liberia's Development

Dreaming of Liberia's development,
More than the development that
Current powerful, more developed countries know,
With homeless people suffering in the cold,
And in the midst of plenty, people are poor.
There, homicides occur every single day,
Amidst claims of being the greatest; that's what they say.

Dreaming of Liberia's development,
Development that helps all children healthily grow,
Development through which education opportunities glow,
Development that helps people stay financially secured,
Development so that security and peace are sustainably ensured,
Development by which human decency always shows,
Development that's better than anything that we've seen before.

But please know that development will not come
Just by dreaming tonight, today, or tomorrow
Nor by claiming to be victims or crying about sorrow;
Development will only come when it is welcomed
Through hard work with dignity and productivity,
Through commitment, determination, and integrity.

For Development to Come to Each of Us

For development to come to each of us,
We should stop making so much fuss
Because fuss only takes us backwards;
If not, it slows our progress forward.
In any case, we'll have to pay a much higher price
As well as make the necessary greater sacrifice
For development to come to each of us,
Which really means leaving no one behind
So that no time is spent going back to find
The causes and sustainable solutions of the fuss
That caused development not to come to each of us.

Liberia's Development Is Under Your Command

Arise, Liberians, work for the development of your land!
Don't forget Liberia's development is under your command,
The vision and dreams for which your old folks toiled;
Build on the foundation they laid long ago.
They used kerosene and palm oil; they burned the midnight oil,
Aiming to build a nation, a task from which they did not recoil
Even though they did some things right and others wrong;
Learning from their experiences today should make us strong.

Today, we have the constitution, modern laws, and bylaws,
But one may, at times, go astray; we are not without flaws.
We must try, try, and try again to develop the land;
As the saying suggests, if at first you do not succeed,
You must try again, hand in hand, work and take a stand!
Don't forget, Liberia's development is under your command.
Never cease to search for all the right clues
To help you understand and do what you must.
Liberia's development is under your command.

Liberia's Wellbeing First

After all is said and done,
Let bygones be bygones
Put Liberia's wellbeing first.
The past is gone in yesteryears.
Let's build a future starting today
To ensure the Liberian ship of State
Sails on calm and peaceful seas.
Let us all, with this resolve,
Work as a united people
And sing along in harmony,
"In union strong, success is sure,"
"All hail, Liberia, hail; all hail"[19]

---

[19]   Quoted from the Liberian National Anthem

Help Us Help Ourselves

Help us help ourselves.
Help us understand Liberia.
Help us to avoid disaster-prone areas.
Help us understand challenging issues
Help us address them by taking the right steps
Help so that others will follow in the right steps.
Help us identify and seize opportunities.
Help us do this in all communities, big and small.
Help us place our interest in our nation.
Help us persevere with the utmost determination.
Help us be full of hope, wisdom, and strength.
Help us stay courageous and strong in the face of adversity.
Help us pick others up when they fall.
Help us open our doors to those seeking shelter within our walls.
Help us keep those within borders secure from others' claws.
Help us help ourselves in all of this with love in our hearts,
And we will forever twinkle like the stars above,
Respecting each other with the greatest love

first

Above All Else

To put Liberia first, above all else; above all else, to put Liberia first
   Above selfish-driven personal ambition
   Above power-driven partisan tradition
   Above corruption-driven temptation
   Above ideology-driven expedience
   Above acts that lead to misfeasance.
To put Liberia first, above all else; above all else, to put Liberia first
   Think and act with human decency
   Think and act with effectiveness and efficiency
   Think and act in ways that achieve proficiency
   Think and act with care, swiftly and proactively
   Think and act, for practical results, innovatively
To put Liberia first, above all else; above all else, to put Liberia first

Taking your Place at The Liberian Table

For the good of Liberia,
Find and take your place at the table,
Not with the intent to eat everything
Or just to talk and do nothing later,
But to contribute to the major things.
In words and deeds, let your actions ring
So, they help others become more able,
To make Liberians more capable,
And increase the size of the table
Upon which more things can be placed
In ways that everyone can embrace.
Find and take your place at the table,
A place where there is an enabling seat
To ensure that everyone will be able to eat
Accountably, in tune with the development beat,
Devoid of all corrupt intent to cheat.

That Dream Can Be Fulfilled

Let Liberia in my dreams
Be a place I can call home,
A home I can truly claim
As mine and only mine alone.
That dream can be fulfilled, I say,
      In simple words, with solid, concrete deeds,
And nothing to fear but their lies and what they breed.

Let Liberia in your dreams,
Be a place you can call your home
A home you can truly claim
As yours and only yours alone.
That dream can be fulfilled, I say.
      In simple words, with solid, concrete deeds,
And nothing to fear but their jealousy and greed.

Let Liberia in our dreams
Be a place that we can all call home,
A home that we can truly claim
As ours and only ours alone.
That dream can be fulfilled, I say
      In simple words, with solid, concrete deeds,
And working with others to meet their needs.

When Liberia is my home,
When Liberia is your home,
When Liberia is our home,
Then your home is my home,
And my home is your home.
That dream can be fulfilled, I say.
      In simple words, with solid, concrete deeds
And nothing to fear—yes, nothing, nothing indeed!

Ebola

Ebola, Ebola, Ebola, Ebola!
I swear o, I swear to my ma; I nah jokin
o'; my peopo, belee me yah
Dar Ebola issue den real; Ebola, you your sef
know it; don sit down dare and preten'
I fear you, yah; we know you wicky; we
know for tru tru who you be
Yea, my man, I tare you tru; yea, everywon, I tare you tru
Ebola is rea; Ebola is righ' here in Libeya; Ebola is baa!
It na goo for nobody; we mus figh' dess Ebola businit well well
We mus kill it now in our country
We mus stop it from spreadin' to other countries dem
A yah Ebola nah goo O[20]

It was in the year twenty fourteen.
I remember it well—it was the year my twin sons turned eighteen.
Ebola, you came to our country uninvited
And you were and still are not welcome.
We are serious; this is no joke or source of fun
We know not from where you came,
Or how, where, or when you got your name.
Some say you're a man-made genetically
modified organism or GMO
Tests to curb your deadly impact have gone
wrong—now there's no cure.
Some say you came from bats and monkeys,
But how did they get it? We don't know!
Ebola, there are other controversy theories
That lead to more and more stories and more and more queries.

---

[20] Liberian jargon expressing the veracity of the existence of Ebola in Liberia, its danger to the country, and the need to contain and, ultimately, obliterate it.

What is the truth, the real truth and nothing
but the truth, we don't know.
But it matters not, because your devastating effects are the same.
All we ask is that you go away.
Yes, leave now! Go! Go! Go!
And cause pain, fear, grief, and death no more.

It is true; you've caused much fear, death, and prolonged grief
You are stealing our livelihood; you're
far worse than an armed thief.
You are doing the same to Guinea and Sierra Leone.
You are a threat to all of Africa's rising continental zones.
The global community is hounded by feelings of gloom
And fear that you could destroy their efforts
toward their recovery boom.

After all, you must know, the world is now a Global Village.
Ebola don't doubt this Village's resolve;
don't dare doubt its courage.
Beware, this Village is launching a global fight
To kick you out far away from our line of sight
To the place of your inglorious demise,
A place darker than a starless night.

Now, back to Liberia, you despicable Ebola,
Know that after our long struggle to end civil wars and insecurity,
You are what threatens our country's
fragile socio-economic stability.
You are creating more challenges in our
fight against widespread poverty.
You are reversing the progress we've made even amidst adversity.
You are no good for our vision for transformation,
development, and tranquility
Ebola know this and know it well; we'll defeat you and gain relief.

We'll attack you left, right, and center and make
your long-intended stay here brief.

Fellow Liberians, for our longevity and
history, we'll leave for posterity.
Our successful fight against Ebola, ultimately
exercising our responsibilities.
Fellow Liberians moving on let us
galvanize our collective abilities.
Let us be focused and explore all possibilities.
Fellow Liberians, let us learn about Ebola and spread the facts,
Even though our efforts to stop Ebola were initially too slow,
Even though the international response was initially low,
Even though we have no source of funding
that would abundantly flow,
Even though we have not the expertise and infrastructural facilities.
How, then, can we beat this unprecedented
epidemic plaquing our nation?
We should do whatever we can, use wisely
our limited resources and abilities
We should do what is good with integrity,
For our nation and all the other affected nations.

The current situation of increasing fear, grief,
and death should set our unity aglow,
With bright lights, enlightening our path toward containing Ebola.
Let us think about the good for Liberia—our one and only nation.
Fellow Liberians, as it is said, "There is a time for everything."
This is not the time for empty criticism with hidden intentions.
This is not the time for baseless accusations.
This is not the time for greed-driven distractions.
This is not the time for politically blinded misdirection.
This is not the time to seek out one's political aims
By calling for a regime change and playing other political games,
By taking massive strike actions that would worsen our situation.

Even though we know you strikers need more than we can mention,
Doing things not in the interest of the common
good of the nation at this time
Will further divide us; we'll only end up being shamed.
Selfishness will tarnish our name; this would only help Ebola win,
Leaving our people to die,
No no no, this is the time for unity, for compassion;
for determination and hard work.
We are one people, one Liberia, no matter where
we originated from; we are the same.

Ebola must know it will die;
Let's ensure this by using well the external help we receive.
Misusing funds for personal gain will make people more aggrieved.
First, we must believe Ebola is real and it's here—believe.
Let's heed the medics and other experts'
advice on what to do and what not to.
This will help kill Ebola, and this will be
good news; indeed, good news.

As for you, Ebola, hear me well; you will die
no matter how you were conceived,
Even with your tendency to replicate, your goal
to destroy us will not be achieved,
Despite all your disguises, as you constantly
mutate, we will not be deceived.
Ebola, you don't know who we are; our efforts
to fight you will soon reap success.
Yes, with hard work and the right attitude, we
will soon be out of this Ebola mess.
Ebola, we will make sure you are vanquished,
and we will not give a damn
Even if you think you have human rights, which would be a sham.
Everything seems to have rights these
days, so you may think you can.

But no, Ebola; you are more inhumane and
destructive than floods from a broken dam.
You have and will never pass the human rights exam.

Liberians, we must contribute to kill Ebola and do all we truly can,
Every able child, every woman, and every man,
Let us all, loud and clear, heed the clarion call,
Together with all Liberians as individuals, one and all,
Together as groups in diaspora like "Rise
Liberia" and "Liberian Awards,"
And like so many others that do not come
to mind now and all the rest,
You know yourselves; let's collaborate in
fighting Ebola and give our best.
Let us move, in unity and with a sense of
purpose, steadfastly forward.
Let us prove that we can pass the "one people, one Liberia" test.
I assure you, Ebola's annihilation in Liberia
and everywhere will be a great reward.
This cannot be emphasized enough; let's
fight together and disregard
All distractions to ensure Ebola's demise,
ensure Ebola will forever disappear,
And ensure it will go deep down under and never rise or reappear

Thin Line

Serendipity may be good at the right time
Stupidity, I have my doubts
But overreliance always on serendipity
Leads one toward the realms of stupidity
Sometimes, there is a thin line between the two
This is a message just for you

So Much in Between

When you always believe that good is bad
And there is nothing between the two,
When you always believe that bad is good,
And there is nothing between the two,
Wonder not why people think you are somehow mad,
Because for them, good is good and bad is bad
And so much is between the two.

What Good are You?

For the development of your home
Ask yourself, what good are you?
You said you had visions,
But know not what you envisioned.
No one else knows, too,
What good are you?
You said you spoke,
But know not what you said.
No one else knows, too,
What good are you?
You said you acted,
But know not what you did.
No one else knows, too,
What good are you?
For the development of your home
Ask yourself, what good are you?
We ask you too,
What good are you?

When Your House Full of Things Falls Apart

When your house full of things falls apart,
Things ill-conceived,
Things wrongly perceived,
Things beyond all possible belief,
Things from which you seek relief,
        Was the top of your house too heavy,
        Or was the foundation not solid enough,
        When your house full of things falls apart?

To Kill the Flies

My friend to be wise
You must open your eyes
That is when you'll really know
The situation we face is not easy
It is like trying, with eyes closed, to kill the flies
That spread the disease like wildfires
So, you'll do much better when you open your eyes
To kill the flies that spread the disease

Diseases like poor education and health; no jobs
Low agriculture output; no industrial production
And many more that have been brought to our attention
The diseases are what hinder poverty reduction
How can we heal these diseases and kill the flies
When many small politicians tell small and big lies
When many big politicians tell all sizes and shades of lies
And so, doing, they make many people cry and cry
Taking things under and behind the table
Claiming they are good people and the ones most able
To kill the flies that spread the diseases

My friend to be wise
You must open your eyes
See those who are truly trying despite the odds
Join them and do more than just praying to God
Dreaming you can do with ease
But it requires much more to heal the diseases
It requires much more to kill the flies
My friend, be wise; open your eyes

Definitely and Infinitely

Find your potential and make use of it.
You think that would be good?
I hope you'll say definitely!
For how long would that be good?
I hope you'll say infinitely!

As long as there are possibilities,
And unbounded opportunities.
At the end of the day,
If what we do is good every day,
The impact will be felt always,
Definitely and infinitely.

The Fight with Mr. Poverty

I don't remember when we met.
All I recall is that I was soaked and wet,
Cold and trembling and full of fright.
My future seemed dark as night,
You were stronger and had the might,
I struggled in that terrible fight.

I survived the danger you posed,
You're Mr. Poverty, with many foes.
You must wonder how I know your name,
You are big and bad, always the same

Now I've survived; I'll keep you in sight.
I'll work against you day and night.
I'll help others, I'll show them the light.
No longer will you be to them a threat.
You'll no longer be my people's plight.
You'll disappear on a one-way flight—
This I believe, and I know I'm right.

The Most Enduring Achievement

In the quest for development,
One can never know all the elements
To enhance the enlightenment
Of the challenges inherent
In making development
The most enduring achievement.
Rather, facilitate the empowerment
Of the people by making them more intelligent
In dealing with the challenges inherent
To make development
The most enduring achievement.
The elders should facilitate the empowerment,
Of the youths to benefit from the age of enlightenment,
Ensuring that they are united in their actions and sentiments
To effectively tackle the elements that cause impediments
To the enduring achievement of development.

Unity in Diversity

The whole as in oneness,
One people from diversity,
All togetherness,
As a necessity
For the conventional phrase
Unity in diversity
True essence of its meaning
To be realized for all our people.
From all parts of our country,
One nation, one people,
One Liberia, one Liberia.
Unity in diversity

The Problems

The problems—
Most were predictable.
But you failed to predict them.
Instead, you spent your time wastefully.
The problems—
Most were preventable.
But you failed to prevent them.
Instead, you spent your time doing the wrong things.
Now you wonder night and day,
Why you have the problems.
You ask others to make the problems go away,
Despite ignoring what earlier they had to say,
On predicting and preventing these problems.
Now what do you really expect from them?
Remember what our elders used to say,
"If you do not hear, you will certainly feel."

The Flame of Development's Fire

Let's light the flame of development's fire
And be ignited with one passionate desire—
To be freed from hatred, greed, and deceit
And other vices that caused our past defeats.
In our fight to be united, developed, and strong,
Let us be fired up with the flame of the development fire.
By so doing, the time to succeed will not be too long
In our fight to be united, developed and strong.

Keeping Ideas and Actions Safe for Everyone

Ideas alone are unlikely to be good enough.
For Liberia's accelerated development,
Ideas must be followed by result-based actions.
Ideas are, however, necessary beginnings.
So, let us strive for an environment
Where there is freedom of speech
To make ideas safe for everyone.
And everyone safe for ideas.
Even if we have to agree to disagree, let civility prevail,
With the hope that whatever actions follow,
Will be good for future ideas and actions
To ensure Liberia's growth and development.

We Are All Liberian People

We are all your people, Liberia.
Whether we were once sold as slaves by our own people,
Whether we were fleeing from the jihads from the North,
Whether the love of liberty brought us here
To seek a new life on your shores,
Whether some of us who later returned
Treated some of us we met here unfairly—
Because we wrongly thought we were superior—
Whether we were always at war with each other,
We are all your people, Liberia.
We together should focus on our future,
A future to correct all the wrongs
And build on the rights and the progress achieved.
We are all Liberian people—here, there or yonder.

Advice

They may call us "country" everywhere we go; just know we are Liberians.
Today and tomorrow, they may call us "Conguh"; just know we are Liberians.
No matter what the situation, we are vital parts of this nation—one Liberia.
No matter if times have changed or remained the same; we are Liberians.
There will be those bent upon calling us names over and over.
They hardly ever do anything else, and when they do, they're negative and clueless.
They sow social discord, breed distrust, and know not what they think they know.
They have no track record of good, concrete things, in words or deeds, that show.
Perhaps, they can restructure their thoughts to promote social inclusiveness.
I say to you, never tire of advising; help others in revising plans and goals
And ways to meet the challenges, challenges in moving all Liberians ahead,
Challenges in helping them overcome the insecurity that makes them afraid,
Challenges in ensuring that their plans do not die like paper on burning coals.

The Struggle and the Strugglers

A struggle wrongly done
Leads to prolonged struggles,
Which are never won,
Not until the strugglers are all gone,
Leaving only the legacy of struggling
And the struggles wrongly done.

Something or Nothing

Sometimes, it's nothing
Whatever we do in life.
"No big deal," that's what they say.
Sometimes, it's something
Whatever we do in life.
"It's just awesome", that's what they say.
In life's ups and downs,
One's life can be nothing or something.
It all depends on what one does,
Something or nothing.
Something wrong and nothing good,
Something good and nothing wrong.

Find Time to Come and Work Together

All Liberians, far and near,
Find time to come and work together.
Help our country make progress,
Meet the ups and downs without fear.
We can do this now, all together.
All Liberians, far and near
Find time to come and work together.

Happenings: Yesterday and Today

Yesterday, this happened to me.

You said you were part of us.
You said you had come just for a while to visit,
Not to cause any palaver, any fuss.
Some said that the way you came was illicit,
Some said you were power-crazy mad,
And that you could be extremely bad.
But you said that was the biggest lie,
You would never even hurt a fly.
Others saw you as a light, a beacon
To do good things for the nation, they reckoned.
And so, with open arms, they said you were welcome.
Later, you said you came for the cause of the people.
You wanted to lead the struggle in a struggle
To redeem a nation, you saw was crippled
Because of factors you said made the nation bleed.
After the struggle, you promised we would all have fun.
But this did not happen—you caused the people to run.
You caused them to cry, to suffer, and to die.
Then you laughed at me as you waved goodbye.
But you did not go far, you could not go far.
The people rose up; they saw your deceit
Today we have reconciled, as one people, one nation,
With no reprisal for the past; we have arisen with determination
To walk on a path that is good for our nation.

Today, this is happening to me.

My Love for Liberia

My love for Liberia
Is not the kind that flows through my blood to my head like wine.
My love for Liberia
Is not the kind that has regular beats like this heart of mine.

My love for Liberia
Is a kind that is real and everlasting, time after time.
My love for Liberia
Is like food, exercise, and good dietary supplements
That fuel human growth and development.

Help Yourself Improve Your Ability

Help yourself improve your ability
To fulfil your responsibilities.
The busybodies will then cease their talking,
As they do nothing but constant stalking
Looking for a chance to criticize,
Casting everything in a negative light.

But you should be positive in your line of sight
Be objectively constructive
That way you can turn what's considered negative
Into what may be considered positive
To help yourself improve your ability
To fulfil your responsibilities

My People Are Beautiful

My people are beautiful.
Perhaps more beautiful than you,
With your well-built appearance
And your angelic face and smiles.

My people are beautiful
In what they say and what they do
And how they say what they say.
My people are beautiful

My people are beautiful
In their disposition and character.
In their judgment and gratitude.
Much more beautiful than you

.

Do Something Good for Liberia

My people hear me well!

You feel, you see, and you do much more.
But time waits for no one; yes, indeed, no one.
That, you've heard; that, I'm sure you know.
But keeping that aside, what have you really done
For Liberia, for its daughters and sons,
For its development now and tomorrow?

Take a break, evaluate yourself.
What have you achieved, what can you claim?
You have dreamed dreams of having fame.
You have expressed, time after time, ambitious aims.
You have talked, talked, and talked about talks.
When questioned, you give excuses, you balk.

Those who know you say nothing is what you do.
You often say your time has not yet come,
But time waits for no one; yes, indeed no one.
Do something now for Liberia, your home.
Do it with a few, do it with many, or do it alone.
But do something good for Liberia now.

My people, I hope you heard me well!

The Conversation

In deep thoughts, Liberia said aloud in the Conversation,

> "I am Liberia and I need development now.
> My land is rich and, yet, I am so very poor.
> Development has been elusive, time after time.
> This is clear, it can be seen in everyone's eyes.
> They tell me to be patient, poverty I'll overcome.
> They say, 'Development is like a slow-growing seed,
> 'It will grow and, in time, meet all my needs.'
> But I say, how long should I wait? I am already old!
> Born in July 26, 1847, that's like another era,
> An era that has floated away in a black hole in space.
> Will development come at a time when I am dead?
> With old age, climate change, terrorism, and other global challenges,
> I may be dead sooner than later, even though I don't wish to ever die.
> All this considered, I need development now; more than ever before.
> I am tired of people eating dry rice, cassava, and bread.
> I am tired of eating just farina and smoke fish
> I am tired of social and physical insecurity.
> I am tired of the lack of good and useful education
> I am tired of poor health, suffering, and pain.
> I am sick and tired of the lack of development."

Participating in the Conversation
Was a little Rice Bird in a breadfruit tree.
The little Rice Bird replied
In a language Liberia could understand,

"Liberia, Liberia, Liberia, I listened to you and I empathize.
Besides internal fighting, criticism, and casting blame,
Besides, playing, most of the time, their political games,
What have your people done, what are they doing?
I mean, what contributions have they made to your development?
What have your people done for you to become developed now?
I mean, things that are truly positive and constructive.
I know that some people are trying hard despite the odds.
I know where you have come from amid challenges and setbacks.
I know a lot has been achieved over time, including the following,
Safeguarding your sovereignty that allows us to sing today.
All hail Liberia! In union, success is sure; we will prevail after all.
In addition, old debts and national integration challenges must be resolved.
Peace, along with a path for stability and better governance, must be secured.
Being transformed from a failed and pariah state classification,
And overcoming so many other socio-economic related hurdles,
So much more, yes, a lot more, needs to be done.
Some people try to do the right things, but sometimes in a wrong way.
I, therefore, understand your desire for development now."

Liberia thoughtfully said, "I hear you well and you raised relevant points to ponder, but it seems you have more to say. Please go ahead; speak in a language that I can understand."

The little Rice Bird continued.

Sitting high in the breadfruit tree.
Loudly and clearly,
In a language Liberia could understand,

> "I know some of your people have good intentions and the will,
> But they don't have what is also important—the required skills.
> Some have the skills but lack knowledge of how to use them.
> Some have the will and the required skills but lack the character—
> A character devoid of corruption, dishonesty, and blatant greed,
> A character without egotistical bigotry and hypocrisy,
> A character lacking a sense of objectivity and true commitment,
> A character pretending to know what is not known,
> A character lacking an understanding of Liberia's ins and outs,
> Yet, casts aspersions on others who do their best in each context,
> A character lacking an understanding of the factors that could raise Liberia,
> A character lacking an understanding of what brings and keeps Liberia down,
> Yet, criticize and condemn others who try to address the issues,
> No matter how difficult the tasks, no matter how limited the resources,
> No matter how external factors beyond one's control exacerbate to the problems."

Then Liberia, seeming impatient, interrupted the little Rice bird and said "you are telling me all what's wrong and I agree but

you are not saying what should be done. I want to hear some
suggestions and I want to hear them now.

The little Rice Bird then shook its head,
And, with sympathy, continued,

> "Work on finding the answers Liberia, with your people;
> work on that real hard.
> All I can say that your people need the will, the skills, and
> the knowledge to use them.
> They need a character, not as an ornament for mere display,
> But to reach good and useful ends in promoting human
> development.
> There may be differences in approach, as no one knows
> everything.
> In such a case, strive to strike the right balance through
> compromise—
> Compromise, with the interest of the nation being
> paramount.
> With that focus, hard work, determination, and in union,
> strong,
> Let them build on what has been achieved and reduce
> negativity.
> Development now is possible, but it must be seen in a
> realistic context.
> It cannot be achieved overnight, but in time, development
> is possible.
> Progress depends on commitment and the right attitude of
> your people.
> Let them embrace constructive criticism and be open to
> constructive dialogue.
> Liberia, I hope you heard me well, because I spoke loud
> and clear
> I spoke in a language that you, Liberia, can understand very
> well."

The Little Rice Bird then flew away, far away, thinking about the Conversation.

Liberia thought for a while and said to herself, "I wonder how my people will respond when I communicate what the little bird just said"

Her thoughts were interrupted by a loud voice which was certainly not the voice of the little bird, saying

"Tell your people to believe that your needs can be met,
but first they must believe; they must strategically plan;
they must mobilize resources, and implement the plan with
honesty, and integrity,
They must do so with responsibility and accountability.
Finally, they must evaluate the results of what they did
And they must adjust where necessary
But first they must believe that all things are possible if they
believe!
And work hard to make their belief come true".

Liberia looked around and saw no one but heard the large voice over and over.

Section Two

Insights On Life, Relationships And Related Issues With Social And Philosophical Overtones

Pure and Simple Math

Keeping up with others is good
If, and only if, what they do is good.
Urging others to keep up with others is good,
In such a case, good plus good equals good.
That is pure and simple math,
The answer to which suggests a good path,
As you travel along the ins and outs
Of Liberia's ups and downs

Keeping up with others is good
If you are up-keeping yourself to be good
To keep up with others in ways that are good
And urging others to do so too; to be good.
In such a case, good plus good times good equals better.
That is pure and simple math,
The answer to which suggests a better path,
As you travel along the ins and outs
Of Liberia's ups and downs

Life Goes On

Robert Frost[21] said that all he has learned about life
He could say in the following three words,
"It goes on."
In other words, life goes on.
By implication, let me say that when one's life stops,
That life will be no longer around,
but "life goes on."
Let me say again, before one life stops,
one should try to leave behind
Good words and deeds to help others so that
Their lives go on.
Like Robert Frost says,
Life goes on.
Be a part of that process,
But let it go on in good and kind ways.

---

[21] Quotation from Robert Frost, "In three words I can sum up everything I've learned about life: it goes on." Source: https://www.goodreads.com/author/quotes/7715.Robert_Frost. He was a celebrated American poet (born March 26; died January 29, 1963).He was popularly known for his deep understanding of human nature and used some of his poems to examine social and philosophical issues. A few of his most famous poems are "The Road Not Taken", "Stopping by Woods on a Snowy Evening" and "Mending Walls".

Ask Me Not How Life Is Treating Me

Ask me not how life is treating me
In Liberia's ups and downs.
Ask me how I am treating Life,
Because that is what I do.
I look at things objectively
Before I criticize,
And when I do, I do so constructively.
I think before I speak.
I weigh the pros and cons before I act.
After which I think of what I've said,
And I examine what I've done.
If bad, I think of ways to make it good.
If good, I think of ways to make it better,
After which I strive to make it the best.
That's how I am treating Life
In Liberia's ups and downs.
So, ask me not how life is treating me—
Ask me how I am treating life.

122

My Beautiful Country in Africa

In my beautiful country in Africa,
Death should not be proud.
The great poet John Donne, warned Death some time ago,

"Death be not proud, though some have called thee
Mighty and dreadfull, for, thou art not soe,
One short sleepe past, we wake eternally,
And death shall be no more; death, thou shalt die."[22]

I say, Death, today you may sit on a throne,
Surrounded by folks, in fear, singing your tone,
But one day you will fall, and you'll be all alone,
As you too will enter your eternal rest,
Leaving folks who are good and striving for the best
To sing the tones of my beautiful country in Africa.

"All hail, Liberia, hail; all hail.
In union success is sure. We cannot fail!
With God above our rights to prove,
we will o'er all prevail!"[23]

---

[22] Culled from the poem "Death be not Proud" by John Donne. The poem is believed to have been written between February and August 1609 and was published posthumously in 1633. He was considered the pre-eminent representative of the metaphysical English poets. He was born January 22,1572 and died March 31,1631. Some of his popular poems were "The Flea", "Death be not Proud" and "The Sun Rising". (Wickipedia).

[23] Culled from the National Anthem of Liberia, lyrics by H. E. Daniel Bashiel Warner (3rd President of the Republic of Liberia, 1864–68) and music by Olmstead Luca.

"The Lone Star forever, the Lone Star forever,
O Long may it float o'er land and o'er sea.
Desert it? No! Never!
Uphold it? Ay ever.
All hail, Lone Star, all hail!"[24]

---

[24] Culled from "The Lone Star Forever," a national song of Liberia composed by H. E. Edwin James Barclay (18th President of the Republic of Liberia; 1930–1944).

In Life's Ups and Downs

In life's ups and downs
Be smart; be strong
Be self-confident and just move along
Sometimes you may have to slow down
Do so without a frown
Look forward to the new dawn
But forget not that life has ups and downs
And sometimes there is a middle ground
Which cannot always easily be found
But always try to be smart and strong
By so doing you'll hardly ever go wrong.

The Sign

I am sure there was a sign
When I started my Liberian journey
After the ins and outs
And the ups and downs.
The sign said, "Exit."
I exited.
Only to find myself in the same place
Where I started my Liberian journey
After the ins and outs
And the ups and downs.
The place from where I exited,
I looked back to re-read the sign.
There was no sign.
I am sure there was a sign
When I started my Liberian journey.

The Youths Should Be Encouraged

The youths should be encouraged
By all those old in age
To pass on their knowledge
and help the youth to manage
this our land with courage

Far Away from the Lights of the City

Have you seen the full moon
In an African village
Far away from the lights of the city
Where people live in bad conditions
What a pity; what a pity
The solution is not just moving to the city

Simply Greed

When having so much is never enough
      Everything you need,
      Everything you want:
      Riches, power, and more power,
      You try to get them, hour after hour.
      The true meaning of your creed,
      You always declare with glee;
      Yet that creed, you unhesitatingly flaunt
      And betray your friends in the quest for more.
      You are dirty minded to your very core
      In your search for more and more;
This is called greed, my friend, simply greed.

Hopes and Goals

Hope without a goal
Will yield nothing to behold;
A goal without hope
Will end up an empty envelope.

Wondering Why

I look at the beautiful sky
Blue and white with shades of gray
Why the sky's beauty is colored that way
Ask the Creator, some folks may say
He is the Great One we must glorify
That's something else, I often wonder why

Demand and Supply of Time

Think about the demand and supply of time.
Know that while you demand more and more,
Procrastination and unproductive use of time,
Is a waste of precious time
Know that time is not in endless supply.
You will never have all the time in the world,
And as the saying goes, "Time waits for no one."

Navigating Common Sense and Knowledge

Navigating commonsense for knowledge
Or navigating knowledge for commonsense
What are we likely to find from such navigation
Just knowledge and commonsense in different forms
With the unknown in between; the ever present unknown
When, how and where to best apply one or the other
But apply them we must; apply them we must
To make a difference, a difference for good in our world

Fulfilling Our Dreams

We stand together for what is right
Great is the struggle; justified our fight
We'll live through life's thunder and storms
We'll never from right to wrong transform
Even if we become weary or ill
Despite all odds, we'll fight on still
To take Liberia over rugged hills
Overcoming hurdles and showing goodwill
Developing our land with passion and skills
Until our dreams are, with honor, fulfilled
A Liberian nation, developed and strong
In peace with dignity, moving along
Let us together resolve to do no wrong
To this place in which we all belong
So, as we sing the joyous holiday songs
During this period in our work and play
Let's do good for Liberia always

Believe in Yourself

It costs too much every day
To heal the pain of yesterday.
It causes you to constantly grieve.
Life is tough, but you are strong.
Believe in yourself, for Liberia's sake, believe!
          Think not about the past alone.
          Such thoughts will prolong your pain.
          Set your goals to higher heights.
          Work hard and maintain that sight.
          The pain will cease, in time, not too long.
If you help yourself along the way
And never ever go astray
In Liberia's ups and downs,
A person of substance you will become,
Believe in yourself, for Liberia's sake, believe!

A Good Liberian Person

To be a good person, a good Liberian person,
Live a good life, meet true humanity's test,
Be concerned, not only for those you love, but for all,
Do so as best as you can
Be sincere, do your very best.
Work hard with honesty, integrity,
And exemplify patriotism, not jingoism,
Let your light shine brightly,
Do good, not because you want to be glorified,
Do what you can and try to do it right
To be a good person, a good Liberian person.

Opportunity Lost can be Found

My friend, I recall not too long ago,
We had the opportunity
To get what we wanted
For Liberia, for Liberia.
Our paths crossed almost always
To get what we wanted
For Liberia, for Liberia.
Then you left and I stayed.
When you returned, I left.
Our paths never crossed again,
Like two parallel lines
Moving in the same direction.
But never meeting; our path never crossed
We never got what we wanted
For Liberia, for Liberia.
We lost the opportunity
But that was then, and this is now.
Opportunities lost can be found,
But we must look hard enough.
Look, look, look and never quit.
Opportunities lost can be found.

I am Who I Truly am

I am who I truly am,
A member of the human race.
Simple, but honorable, a Liberian
Moving at my own pace.

Heaven knows I am no angel,
Neither do I worship anyone—
Those with whom I mingle,
On our earthly shores
Those with whom I have no connections.
Wherever else they are

Hell knows I'm no friend of the devil,
Neither do I hang out with anyone—
Those who are pathologically evil,
Those filled with abomination.

I am just a part of humanity
Determined not to compromise
My long-cherished integrity,
Even when I am criticized.

I am simple but honorable—a Liberian.
I keenly listen when Liberia calls.
I am who I truly am.
For Liberia, I'll always stand tall.

Not Religious, not Political

I am not religious; I am not political.
My relationship with god is between me and god.
My relationship with the devil is no relation at all.
Though some may think this view is flawed,
That's how I listen when Liberia calls.

My Friends in Words and Deeds

(Dedicated to all my friends)

My life's momentous encounters
Have led to the friends I have.
So many that I won't name any.
As I've said several times before,
Beginning so many years ago,
We may have different backgrounds,
But just look around us—all around.
You'll see that our friendship is profound.
It's like a straight line that never bends.
Examine it from end to end.
We express our views without fear,
No matter the prevailing atmosphere.
We sometimes agree to disagree,
But we do so with mutual respect.
My friends know that I have their backs,
And I know that they always have mine.
We help each other all the time.
As long as we are able to do so,
We never ever say to each other, "No."
Unless there is a bad thing that most of us know,
We don't hide what it is—we let it show.
We are open and honest with friend or with foe.
Our friendship is like a bright star,
Shining in Africa's night sky, near and far,
It shows us the way we are,
Just the way we are.

My Brothers and Sisters Everywhere

(Dedicated to all my brothers and sisters)

My dear brothers and sisters everywhere
Some from the same mother
Some from the same father
Some just love that ties us together

We have strong shoulders to lean on
Big eyes to see and wide ears to hear
About the burdens we sometimes bear
And all those things that we often fear

But people should never ever be surprise
While we are all in different fields
We protect each other like solid shields
So, our togetherness is strongly sealed

As we enjoy life, despite the ups and downs
I am sure you all will agree that it is true
That I sincerely love you
And just the same, you love me too

Paternal Advice

(Dedicated to Edwin and Erwin Barclay)

I know that you like to be cool,
Wearing "brand named" clothes and expensive shoes,
But in life, it takes much more,
Like waking up in time so as not to be late for school,
Studying hard and earning good grades,
Being focused and serious about school,
Striking the right balance between schoolwork, rest, and play,
Giving your best to earn good grades as a golden rule,
That will help you qualify for professional trades.
So, as time passes, the night, evening, and the day
When people see you as just being cool,
Let them not think that you have a head empty as a mule
And are virtually as useless as a broken tool.
Let them know that you are a person of substance
By the content of your character and intelligence,
By being a person with knowledge and dignified eminence
And not an empty-headed person with arrogance.
I know, yes, I truly know that you are no fool,
So please be focused, succeed in school,
Not only to make me proud, but for your own good.
Let the search for knowledge be as your need for food.
I know that you like to be cool.
Do so by being smart and serious with school.
This is a message from your dad, just for you,
Because he loves you and knows you love him too.

142

In Celebration

(Dedicated to the memories of Bishop Mai Barclay Roberts of the Faith Healing Temple
of Jesus Christ. This poem was initially written as a tribute for the 40th anniversary of the
Faith Healing Temple of Jesus Christ)

O how time passes by, as it does time after time.
Just as the world turns around, around, and around.
The Faith Healing Temple of Jesus Christ
Always strives to stand on solid ground,
Proclaiming the Word and pursuing the quest,
For redemption and, thereby, quenching our thirst
With water from Heaven's well, which never goes
dry
Even in dry seasons, no matter how hard Satan may
try.
The Faith Healing Temple of Jesus Christ
Encourages us to live good lives in the name of
Jesus
To heed His word, to be saved, and to be redeemed
Bravo! The Faith Healing Temple of Jesus Christ

As time passes, day by day and night by night,
Today is a glorious and very special day
For the Faith Healing Temple of Jesus Christ.
It continues to grow along the way,
Helping us place our trust in God first,
Praying that our sinful ways are reversed.
Today is its anniversary—its 40th anniversary.
May it have everything that's necessary,
As a computer having all its accessories.
Of course, with God's merciful blessings,
To meet the challenges, even those not pressing.
Bravo! The Faith Healing Temple of Jesus Christ

Early Departure

(Dedicated to the loving memory of the late Gerald Kwabena
Barclay my grand nephew, who left us in his infancy)

My little grandnephew with such a loving face,
You no doubt came from an ebony black noble race,
From Africa's West Coast, filled with rich grains and gold,
Where our ancestors lived to a ripe golden age,
Ripe like Liberia's grains that, in abundance, flowed,
Golden like Ghana's rich solid gold.
Yes, places called the Grain Coast and the Gold Coast,
The great domains of your parental heritage.
It's tragic that your arrival had problems from the start.
Were you an unfinished work of a future treasured art?
Is that why you left, to finish the unfinished part?
That's what it seems to us so clearly,
Since you left in infancy; yes, so early,
Leaving us in grief, with eyes sad and teary.
Whatever it is, we will remember you always,
Minute by minute, hour by hour, every day,
Week by week, monthly, quarterly, and yearly.
One day, we will see again your loving face.
We'll hold you in that sweet loving African embrace.
For now, rest in peace in that Heavenly place,
My little grandnephew with such a loving face.

A Boy and a Girl

(Dedicated to my son and daughter, Sam and Gloria Barclay-Morris)

Gloria and Samuel,
Our children from Liberia,
A land that has seen hysteria
On the path to meet the criteria
Of development and prosperity.

        Gloria and Samuel,
        I hear you two bathed in true love,
        Blessed by the One believed to be above,
        Just had children one by one—a boy and a girl—
        With beautiful nappy hair and curls.

I truly consider children loving gifts—
A double bundle of joy I can uplift.
I promise to help with their upbringing.
I'll help babysit whenever convenient
And, at a few other times, when inconvenient.

        They will always hear me singing
        Words of the poems I've been composing.
        When I die and go to the great beyond,
        The words and melody will keep ringing.
        Gloria and Sam, it will be profound.

I pray they grow up well and join Ansu and Kobie,
My other loving grandkids, who are growing,
To help improve Liberia's profile
In meeting the several criteria
In every socio-economic area
To attain development and prosperity.

Advice to Little Anthony

(Dedicated to my grandson Anthony Movell Barclay)

Your father is the son of the man
Who happens to be my father's son.
These words were said by someone else
In a different context, but now,
It applies to my own context.
We all are like birds of a feather.
We'll make it in any weather—
Under the rising or falling sun,
Under heavy or drizzling rain.
Liberia is part of us, and so it will remain,
Like the rich red blood flowing in our veins.
We'll make sure our living is not ever in vain.

I know you have ties to the "great and strong" America
But also, to the "well-endowed and resilient" Africa.
More specific for the ties that bind you to Liberia and the USA,
The tri- colors—the red, white, and blue—
Are doubled in more ways than one to you.
You have one large, white sparkling star.
You have over fifty white shining stars,
All cast in different but rich deep blue fields,
With multiple stripes colored red and white.
May they all inspire you to face this life,
With all its daunting and challenging strife.

Use well your God-given strategic might.
Stay strong in the dark and in the light.
Do nothing merely as a reprisal for the past.
Do good things that will eventually last.
Be realistic—in life we all face different kinds of aches,
Sometimes due to our own mistakes.

If your mistakes affect others, never be
too proud to say, "I'm sorry."
Do this with honesty and not in ways that are fake.
Have a clear conscience; don't suffer with prolonged worry,
Causing you to have a perpetual frown
This, my grandson, will definitely take you down.
Amid life challenges, find the time to have fun.
That's how the great battle of life is won.
In every case, as it is often said, "To your own self be true,"
And "Do unto others as you would like them do to you."

Never be the first to start a violent fight,
But as the case may be, stand your ground.
Seize strategic opportunities to look around,
And be prepared to fight with all your might
To do what's necessary from a place of strength,
While keeping your antagonist at an arms' length,
With humanity goals in sight,
Guided by God's help in doing what's right.
After it all, forgive—that's what makes might right.
Little Anthony, after all is said and done,
Always strive to know yourself better and better,
And let "your conscience be your guide" to the letter.

The Arrival

(Dedicated to my son and daughter, Ken and Wiatta Barlay- Wilcox)

I have just received the good news, which I cherish with glee.
In the flesh, I would like to show my smile for all to see.
My lovely little grandson has arrived, healthy and strong.
He arrived not long after my lovely granddaughter came along.
I pray that their lives be productive and prolonged.
They arrived now, when the world is mixed with joy and sorrow.
Beauty abounds, but ugliness constantly shows its face of terror.
I trust they will do what they can, when older, a few years from tomorrow
To strengthen unity in our world and minimize the insanity
To demonstrate in their lives and others the essence of humanity.
Thank you, Ken and Wiatta, my loving kids, for given me these grandkids.
I'll cherish them with love; all potential harm to them God will forbid.

My Love Has No Boundaries For My "Grandies"

(Dedicated to all my grand and great grandchildren)

For my many grand and great grand relatives
Words alone cannot adequately be descriptive
Of how much I love you; you are so sweet
Even those of you I still look forward to meet
My love has no boundaries for each and all of you

Those brought into this world by my own and very own
Not known to some folks but to others they are well known
They are your parents who are always
there for me like my backbone
Yusu, Patience, Charis, Fredie B, and Teetee,
Saydah, Max, Mywen, Charleslyn, and Weewee,
Glennis, Sagbe-Kla, Tomah, Raphael and Leslie
As well as all the rest not mentioned here
Including nephews, nieces, cousins and friends
To list them all will be hard for me to end

I have much to say my "grandies", but I'll just summarize
I hope that you'll grow up to be good, strong, healthy and wise
To deal with the ups and downs in our world today
And with those of tomorrow, rain or shine, everyday
Be honest with yourself and in what you say and do

What causes the ups and downs, may not always show
And as such, some of the things, you may never know
But this I know, and I am certain, yes, I know for sure
Some people are deceitful, mean, untrustworthy and low
But as Michelle Obama says, when folks go low, you go high
I add to say when they are mean you do what's best to be kind
And never fail to think before acting on what first comes to mind.

My Own

In my own yard
Where I treat you as my own
I sit and look at you
Arranging my own cards
To deal me a dirty hand
For reasons to me unknown

Simply Me

I have no hate, no qualms, no greed
My mind, my heart, my soul is free
I have a kind and loving creed
To treat all human beings alike
And not to be the first to strike
Get to know me, and then you'll see
After which you'll, in time, agree
My mind, my heart, my soul is free
As I keep Liberia on my mind
In search for ways for me to find
So, Liberia will never fall behind
That's why I've a kind and loving creed
And have no hate, no qualms, no greed

Nahn Ma Yah

(a consolatory dedication to Arthur Trispin Nickerson, January 2012)

Nick, my Liberian friend and brother
Right now, I can think of no other
During this time of your bereavement
The sadness, the burden, the pain
Like bundles of thorns sticking you again and again
Losing three family members; three love ones
So close proximity in time; almost at once
I know no words can assuage your grief
No amount of money can bring you relief
But I've composed this poem to say in brief
Life has its "ups and downs"
For you this is certainly a "down"
But rest assured it won't last for long
I express my sympathy
In sincere empathy
Believe me, in your situation, I truly care
And in my mind, your sorrow I share
I trust that you'll be strong
With resilience to move ahead; yes, to move along
Overcoming the negativity of bereavement
With the positivity of mind ahead for achievement
I now close with heartfelt feelings to say
In our true traditional Liberian way
Nick, "my brodah, nahn ma yah; nahn ma yah".

This Woman Will Be Remembered

(Dedicated to President Ellen Johnson Sirleaf)

This woman will be remembered
In Liberia's Ups and Downs
Once a child destined to be great
Not only by her will to succeed
The many laurels she received
The battles she fought and won
Believing one for all and all for one

This woman will be remembered
In Liberia's Ups and Downs
Not only when she acquiesced to fight another day
The times she said what she had to say
Despite the odds of what was at play

This woman will be remembered
In Liberia's Ups and Downs
Not only because she deprived no one the right to serve
Related by blood, friendship or politics
The right to serve, she thought they all deserved
As long it was not illegal, she showed the nerve
Competence was a high factor in her choice
Not those who claimed to know by causing noise

If in serving, you betray her and the people's trust
With the habit of repeatedly causing palaver
And making excuses and failing to deliver
Or being deceitful and driven by greed and other ruse
As such, she felt that you'll be destined to most likely lose
Posing a threat to Liberia's progress like a lighted fuse

In such case she did not give a damn
Whether you were a woman or a man
In strategizing how to change the scene
Winning for Liberia was her main thing
She tried to do what was fair and right
To move Liberia ahead within the line of sight

She did not in every case succeed
And she was not too proud to concede
Sometimes things were beyond her control
Sometimes measures she took in the political arena
Deemed inappropriate by partisans caused ripples and rifts
And thus, distractions in making Liberian politics cleaner
Sometimes things, from oversight, did go astray
In each case she never quit thinking to find a better way

Sometimes she had to compromise
As she was not trying to create a paradise
Rather she was just trying to move Liberia forward
Away from the mistakes that took us backwards

She worked to ensure that Liberia would not be left behind
She never claimed to know it all and is by no means divine,
She is only human, but a very special human
This woman will be remembered
In Liberia's Ups and Downs

When Bea Barclay Remembers

(Dedicated to Mrs. Beatrice Barclay)

When Bea Barclay remembers
You will never ever slumber
Her melodies and sweet lyrics
The dances with wild gyrations
Rekindle memories of the nation
Its people and institutions
The good old days and the bad
That made us all glad or sad
When Bea Barclay remembers
No matter what's your gender
You will also remember
Liberia; Liberia; Liberia
And join in as a band member
To sing her song "I remember"
When Bea Barclay remembers

The Restaurant Story

One day I was very hungry,
So, I went to a restaurant
Where the service was slow.
I complained that all would know.
A lady came to me and said,
In measured syllabic words,
"This - is - a - rest-au-rant,
Not - a - fast - food – joint.
So, rest a while and stop the noise.
You came here by your own choice."
To my surprise, she continued,
"Did you see a sign here that says,
'Food is ready, 'Food is ready'?
Go to the cook shops called 'lappa be dor.'
This - is - a - rest-au-rant, my man.
So, rest a while and stop the noise.
You came here by your own choice.
Your food is being prepared.
While you wait, have a drink
That may cause you to not think
That our restaurant is slow.
My man, enjoy the Liberian way, enjoy."
The Liberian way? I wondered and pondered
What is this Liberian way; what is this Liberian way?
And then I lost my appetite as the drink took its toll.

Christmas Day is Here Again

Christmas day is here again.
Let's enjoy and strive to gain
The best life has to offer
After the hard times and pain
Let's ensure we no longer suffer
Put the worries behind us.
All it does is cause stress,
Leaving us in more distress.
Understand this point of view.
Be merry, and I'll join you too
Have some hot soup and fufu,[25]
Or do what you want to do.
Christmas day is here again.
Enjoy it, and let's remain
Peaceful in all domains
In every talk and walk of life.
That is what I truly mean
When I say Christmas day has come again.

---

[25] A stable food, made from cassava; it is common in Liberia and other West African Countries.

Lightning Source UK Ltd.
Milton Keynes UK
UKHW011849210220
359150UK00001B/46/J